Excel VBA

A Step-by-Step Comprehensive Guide on Excel VBA Programming Tips and Tricks for Effective Strategies

PETER BRADLEY

© Copyright 2019 - Peter Bradley - All rights reserved.

The contents of this book may not be reproduced, duplicated or transmitted without direct written permission from the author.

Under no circumstances will any legal responsibility or blame be held against the publisher for any reparation, damages, or monetary loss due to the information herein, either directly or indirectly.

Legal Notice:

This book is copyright protected. This is only for personal use. You cannot amend, distribute, sell, use, quote or paraphrase any part of the content within this book without the consent of the author.

Disclaimer Notice:

Please note the information contained within this document is for educational and entertainment purposes only. Every attempt has been made to provide accurate, up to date and reliable, complete information. No warranties of any kind are expressed or implied. Readers acknowledge that the author is not engaging in the rendering of legal, financial, medical or professional advice. The content of this book has been derived from various sources. Please consult a licensed professional before attempting any techniques outlined in this book.

By reading this document, the reader agrees that under no circumstances is the author responsible for any losses, direct or indirect, which are incurred as a result of the use of information contained within this document, including, but not limited to, —errors, omissions, or inaccuracies.

TABLE OF CONTENTS

Introduction 1

Chapter One: Facts about VBA 2

    Making macros available on every MS Excel Worksheet 2

    Types Of Codes Found Across The Internet 2

    Where To Use The Code You Find On The Internet 3

    Saving A Workbook 3

Chapter Two: Resources for VBA Help 4

    Allow Excel to Write the Code for You 4

    The Location Matters When You Ask For Help 5

    Choose Online Help over Offline Help 5

    Using Code for Excel VBA from the Internet 5

    Making Use of Excel VBA Forums 6

    Visiting Excel VBA Expert Blogs 7

    Mining YouTube for Some Excel VBA Training Videos 8

    Attending a Live Online Excel VBA Training Class 9

    Dissecting Other Excel Files in Your Organization 9

    Ask the Local Excel Guru 10

Chapter Three: How to Improve the Performance of Macros ... 11

    Close Everything Except for the VBA Essentials 11

    Removing Unnecessary Selects 14

Using the With Statement to Read Object Properties.................. 14

Using Arrays And Ranges 15

Use .Value2 Instead Of .Text or .Value 17

Avoid Using Copy and Paste 17

Use The Option Explicit Keyword To Catch Undeclared Variables 19

Chapter Four: Some Problems with Spreadsheets and How to Overcome Them 20

Multi-User Editing 20

Shared Workbooks.. 21

Linked Workbooks 22

Data Validation 23

Navigation Issues 24

Security Issues... 24

Speed Issues.. 24

Enter the database.. 25

Chapter Five: Sub Procedures 29

What Is A Sub Procedure? 29

How Does The VBA Sub Procedure Look? 30

How to Name A VBA Sub Procedure... 33

How to Determine the Scope of A VBA Sub Procedure............... 34

How to Execute / Run / Call a VBA Sub Procedure...................... 39

Option One: How to Execute A VBA Sub Procedure Directly From the Visual Basic Editor.. 39

Option Two: How to Execute A VBA Sub Procedure Using the Macro Dialog 42

Option Three: How to Execute A VBA Sub Procedure
Using a Keyboard Shortcut 46

Option Four: How to Execute A VBA Sub Procedure
Using a Button or Other Object 49

Option Five: How to Execute A VBA Sub Procedure
from another Procedure 61

Option Six: How to Execute A VBA Sub Procedure
Using the Ribbon 73

Option Seven: How to Execute A VBA Sub Procedure
Using the Quick Access Toolbar 84

Option Eight: How to Execute A VBA Sub Procedure
When a Particular Event Occurs 91

Option Nine: Executing the VBA Sub Procedure
Using the Immediate Window 92

Conclusion **94**

Will You Help Me?...**95**

Sources..**97**

Introduction

I want to thank you for choosing this book, *Excel VBA - A Step-by-Step Comprehensive Guide on Excel VBA Programming Tips and Tricks for Effective Strategies'* and hope you find the book informative to learn Excel VBA.

It is difficult for a person to become an expert in VBA within a matter of days. It takes patience, time and practice to master coding in VBA. The first few books of the series provided information on different parts of Excel VBA. You learnt about the different data types, functions and methods you can use in Excel VBA. You also covered information on how you can handle errors and exceptions in VBA using the compiler and the visual basic environment.

There are still some topics that you will need to familiarize yourself with if you want to master coding in VBA. This book covers some of those topics. As a programmer, you will use the words procedures and sub procedures numerous times. This is because you will only be working on building and writing code for sub procedures. This book will provide information on what a sub procedure is, and how you can develop one for your project. You will also gather information on some tips and tricks that you can use to improve the project that you develop.

There are times when your system will slow down because of the volume of data, or code. In such situations, you can use some of the tips mentioned in this book to improve the performance of your project.

Thank you for purchasing the book. I hope you gathered all the information you were looking for.

Chapter One

Facts about VBA

Unlike the usual programming languages with only take code to build a program, we can record actions in VBA using the macro recorder. This has been covered extensively in the previous books. This chapter covers some important facts about macros and VBA.

Making macros available on every MS Excel Worksheet

When you begin to record a macro in VBA, Excel will prompt you to save the macro in a specific location. You can choose from the following locations: the workbook you are writing the macro in or the common workbook. If you save the macro in the current workbook, it will not be available for any other user to use in a different workbook. If you want to use a single macro or procedure across different workbooks, you should save it in personal.xlsb.

The personal.xlsb workbook is a hidden file, and cannot be seen or edited unless you unhide the file. You can view the file when you choose to look at all files in an Excel window.

Types Of Codes Found Across The Internet

You will come across three types of macros across the internet. The first type is the sub() macro. This is a macro that will run and execute a block of code or statements. This is the most common macro type available on the internet.

The second type is a function. This function is like the function that you use in excel, but unlike Excel functions, it is a user defined function. This function will also use VBA code.

The third type of macro is an event procedure that will work only when a certain event occurs. A macro which runs the moment you open your workbook is a classic example of this this type of macro.

You can choose a macro depending on what you want to another. For example, you can record a macro and use a shortcut key to call it when you want to format some cells. Alternatively, you can define a formula within a macro and store it in your files.

Where To Use The Code You Find On The Internet

You must remember to place the coffee write or source in the right place. If you do not save it correctly, it will not work. You can add functions and subs to the modules in your workbook. If you want to insert a module, go to Insert -> Module. Select the module that you want to insert, click it to open it and paste the code. You can include multiple codes in the same module. For some events, you will need to place a macro in the same sheet.

Saving A Workbook

You should always remember to save a workbook as a macro enabled workbook. A sheet that contains a macro will have different properties when compared to a sheet that does not have a macro. If you need to save the workbook as a macro enabled workbook, you should choose to save the workbook in the xlsm format.

Chapter Two

Resources for VBA Help

You cannot expect to become a VBA expert in a day. It is a journey and you will need to practice a lot before you become an expert. The best part about coding in Excel VBA is that there are many resources that you can use to improve your knowledge in Excel. This chapter covers some of the best places you can visit and some of the best resources you can use if you need a push in the right direction.

Allow Excel to Write the Code for You

If you have read the previous books, you know that you can use the macro recorder to help you with understanding your code. When you record any macro or the steps you want to automate using a record macro, Excel will write the underlying code for you. Once you record the code, you can review it and see what the recorder has done. You can then convert the code that the recorder has written into something that will suit your needs.

For instance, if you need to write a macro to refresh a pivot table or all pivot tables in your workbook and clear all the filters in the pivot table, it will get difficult to write the code from scratch. You can instead start recording the macro, and refresh every pivot table and remove all the filters yourself. When you stop recording the macro, you can review it and make the necessary changes to the code.

For a new Excel user, it would seem that the Help system is an add-in that always returns a list of topics that do not have anything to do with the topic you are looking for. The truth is that when you learn how to use the Help System correctly, it is the easiest and the fastest way to obtain more information about a topic. There are two basic tenets that you must keep in mind:

The Location Matters When You Ask For Help

There are two Help Systems in Excel – one that provides help on the different features in Excel and the other that provides information on some VBA programming topics. Excel will not perform a global search but will throw the criteria against the Help system, which is in your current location. This means that you will receive the help that you need depending on which area of Excel you are working in. If you want help on VBA and macros, you need to be in the Visual Basic Environment (VBE) when you look for information. This will ensure that the keyword search is performed on the correct help system.

Choose Online Help over Offline Help

When you look for some information on a topic, Excel will see if you are connected to the internet. If your system is connected to the internet, Excel will return results using some online content on Microsoft's website. Otherwise, Excel will use the help files that are stored offline in Microsoft office. It is always good to choose online help since the content is more detailed. It also includes updated information and the links to other resources that you can use.

Using Code for Excel VBA from the Internet

The secret about coding or programming is that there is no necessity to build original code. The macro syntax that you need to use is always available on the internet. This proves that there is no need to create or develop code from scratch. You can use some existing code on the internet and then apply the code to a specific scenario.

If you are stuck with creating or writing a macro for a specific task, all you need to do is describe the task you want to accomplish using

Google Search. All you need to do is add the words "Excel VBA" before you describe your requirement.

For instance, if you want to write a macro to delete every blank row in a worksheet, you should look for, "How to delete blank rows in a worksheet in Excel VBA?" You can bet a whole years' worth of salary that a programmer has already developed code for the same problem. There is probably an example that is available on the internet, which will give you an idea of what you need to do. This way you can simply build your own macro.

Making Use of Excel VBA Forums

If you find yourself in a spot, and are unsure of what to do, you should post a question on a forum. The experts on these forums will guide you based on your requirement. A user forum is an online community that revolves around specific topics. You can ask numerous questions in these forums and get advice from experts on how you should solve some problems. The people answering your questions are volunteers who are passionate about helping the Excel community solve some real-world problems.

Many forums were built or developed to helping people with Excel. If you want to find such a forum, you should type "Excel Forum" in Google Search. Let us look at some tips you can use to get the most out of the user form.

You should always read the forum and follow all the rules before you begin. These rules will often include some advice on how you should post your questions and also the etiquette you should follow.

Always check if the question you want to ask has already been answered. You should try to save some time by looking at the archives. Now, take a moment to look at the forum and verify if any of the questions you want answers to have already been asked.

You should use accurate and concise titles for any of your questions. You should never create a forum question using an abstract title like "Please Help" or "Need advice."

You should always ensure that the scope of your question is narrow. You should never ask vague questions like "Can I build an accounting tool in Excel?"

You should always be patient, and remember that the people who are trying to answer your question also have a day job. You should always give the experts time to answer the questions.

You should always check often when you post your questions. You will probably receive some information when they will ask you to provide some information about your question. Therefore, you should always return to your post to either respond to some questions or review the answer.

You should always thank the person who has answered your question. If the answer helps you, you should let the expert know the same.

Visiting Excel VBA Expert Blogs

Some Excel Gurus have shared their knowledge about VBA on their blogs. These blogs have a large number of tips and tricks that you can use to improve your VBA skills. They have some information that you can use to build your skills. The best part of using these blogs is that they are free to use.

These blogs do not necessarily answer your specific questions, but they offer many articles that you can use to advance your knowledge of VBA and Excel. These blogs can also provide some general guidance on how you can apply Excel in different situations. Let us look at a few popular Excel blogs:

ExcelGuru

ExcelGuru is a blog that was set up by Ken Puls. He is an Excel expert who shares all his knowledge on his blog. Apart from the blog, Ken also offers many learning resources you can use to improve your knowledge in Excel.

Org

Org is a blog that was set up by Purna Chandoo Duggirala. He is an Excel expert from India who joined the scene in 2007. His blog offers innovative solutions and some free templates that will make you an Excel expert.

Contextures

Debra Dalgleish is the owner of a popular Excel website and is great with Microsoft Excel. Se has included close to 350 topics on her website, and there will definitely be something that you can read.

DailyDose

The DailyDose is a blog that is owned by Dick Kusleika. It is the longest running Excel blog, and Dick is an expert at Excel VBA. He has written articles and blogs for over ten years.

MrExcel

Bill Jelen always uses Excel to solve any problems he has at work. He offers a large archive of training resources and over thousands of free videos.

Mining YouTube for Some Excel VBA Training Videos

If you know that there are some training videos that are available on the internet, and these sessions are better than articles, you should look for those videos. There are many channels that are run by amazing experts that are passionate for sharing knowledge. You will be pleasantly surprised to see the quality of those videos.

Attending a Live Online Excel VBA Training Class

Live training sessions are a great way to absorb good Excel knowledge form a diverse set of people. The instructor is providing some information on different techniques, but the discussions held after the class will leave you with a wealth of ideas and tips. You may have never thought of these ideas ever before. If you can survive these classes, you should always consider attending more of these sessions. Here are some websites that you can use for such sessions:

1. Org
2. ExcelHero
3. ExcelJet
4. Learning From The Microsoft Office Developer Center For Help With VBA

You should use the Microsoft Office Dev Center to get some help on how to start programming in Office products. The website is slightly difficult to navigate, but it is worth it to look at the sample code, free resources, step-by-step instructions, tools and much more.

Dissecting Other Excel Files in Your Organization

Previous employees or current employees may have created files that already answer some of your questions. You should try to open different Excel files that contain the right macros, and also look at how these macros function. Then see how other employees in the organization develop macros for different applications. You should try not to go through the macro line-by-line but should look for some new techniques that may have been used.

You can also try to identify new tricks that you may have never thought of. You will probably also stumble upon some large chunks of code that you can implement or copy into your workbooks.

Ask the Local Excel Guru

Is there an excel genius in your department, company, community or organization? If yes, you should become friends with that person now. That person will become your own personal guru. Excel experts love to share their knowledge, so you should never be afraid to approach an expert if you have any questions or want to seek advice on how you can solve some problems.

Chapter Three

How to Improve the Performance of Macros

There are times when VBA will run very slowly, and this is certainly frustrating. The good news is that there are some steps that you can take to improve the performance of the macro. This chapter will provide some information on the different steps you should take to improve the speed and performance of a macro. Regardless of whether you are an IT administrator, end user or a developer, you can use these tips to your benefit.

Close Everything Except for the VBA Essentials

The first thing to do to improve the performance of VBA is to turn off all the unnecessary features like screen updating, animation, automatic events and calculations when the macro runs. All these features will always add an extra overhead, which will slow the macro down. This always happens when the macro needs to modify or change many cells and trigger a lot of recalculations or screen updates.

The code below will show you how you can enable or disable the following:

- Animations
- Screen updates
- Manual Calculations

```vba
Option Explicit

    Dim lCalcSave As Long

    Dim bScreenUpdate As Boolean

    Sub SwitchOff(bSwitchOff As Boolean)

     Dim ws As Worksheet

     With Application

      If bSwitchOff Then

       ' OFF

       lCalcSave = .Calculation

      bScreenUpdate = .ScreenUpdating

       .Calculation = xlCalculationManual

       .ScreenUpdating = False

       .EnableAnimations = False

       '

       ' switch off display pagebreaks for all worksheets

       '

       For Each ws In ActiveWorkbook.Worksheets

        ws.DisplayPageBreaks = False

       Next ws

      Else

       ' ON
```

```
        If .Calculation <> lCalcSave And lCalcSave <> 0 Then
.Calculation = lCalcSave

        .ScreenUpdating = bScreenUpdate

        .EnableAnimations = True

      End If

      End With

    End Sub

    Sub Main()

      SwitchOff(True) ' turn off these features

      MyFunction() ' do your processing here

      SwitchOff(False) ' turn these features back on

    End Sub
```

Disabling All The Animations Using System Settings

You can disable animations through the Ease of Access center in Windows. You can use this center to disable some specific features in Excel by going to the Ease of Access or Advanced Tabs on the menu. For more information, please use the following link: https://support.office.com/en-us/article/turn-off-office-animations-9ee5c4d2-d144-4fd2-b670-22cef9fa

Disabling Office Animations Using Registry Settings

You can always disable office animations on different computers by changing the appropriate registry key using a group policy setting.

HIVE: HKEY_CURRENT_USER

Key Path: Software\Microsoft\Office\16.0\Common\Graphics

Key Name: DisableAnimations

Value type: REG_DWORD

Value data: 0x00000001 (1)

If you use the Registry Editor incorrectly, you can cause some serious problems across the system. You may need to re-install Windows to use the editor correctly. Microsoft will help you solve the problems of a Registry Editor, but you should use this tool if you are willing to take the risk.

Removing Unnecessary Selects

Most people use the select method in the VBA code, but they add it in places where it is not necessary to use them. This keyword will trigger some cell events like conditional formatting and animations, which will hinder the performance of the macro. If you remove all the unnecessary selects, you can improve the performance of the macro. The following example will show you the code before and after you make a change to remove all the extra selects.

Before

```
Sheets("Order Details").Select

Columns("AC:AH").Select

Selection.ClearContents
```

After

```
Sheets("Order Details").Columns("AC:AH").ClearContents
```

Using the With Statement to Read Object Properties

When you work with objects, you should the With statement to decrease the number of times that the compiler reads the properties of the object. In the example below, see how the code changes when you use the With statement.

Before

> Range("A1").Value = "Hello"
>
> Range("A1").Font.Name = "Calibri"
>
> Range("A1").Font.Bold = True
>
> Range("A1").HorizontalAlignment = xlCenter

After

> With Range("A1")
>
>   .Value2 = "Hello"
>
>   .HorizontalAlignment = xlCenter
>
>   With .Font
>
>   .Name = "Calibri"
>
>   .Bold = True
>
>   End With
>
> End With

Using Arrays And Ranges

It is expensive to read and write to cells every time in Excel using VBA. You incur an overhead every time there is some movement of data between Excel and VBA. This means that you should always reduce the number of times the data moves between Excel and VBA. It is at such a time that ranges are useful. Instead of writing or reading the data individually to every cell within a loop, you can simply read the entire range into an array, and use that array in the loop. The example below will show you how you can use a range to read and write the values at once without having to read each cell individually.

```vb
Dim vArray As Variant

Dim iRow As Integer

Dim iCol As Integer

Dim dValue As Double

vArray = Range("A1:C10000").Value2 ' read all the values at once from the Excel cells, put into an array

For iRow = LBound(vArray, 1) To UBound(vArray, 1)

  For iCol = LBound(vArray, 2) To UBound(vArray, 2)

    dValue = vArray (iRow, iCol)

    If dValue > 0 Then

      dValue=dValue*dValue ' Change the values in the array, not the cells

      vArray(iRow, iCol) = dValue

    End If

  Next iCol

Next iRow

Range("A1:C10000").Value2 = vArray ' writes all the results back to the range at once
```

Use .Value2 Instead Of .Text or .Value

You can retrieve your values in different ways from a cell. The property you use to retrieve that information will have an impact on the performance of your code.

.Text

Most programmers use the .Text value to retrieve only the information from a cell. The property will return the formatted value of the cell. It takes a lot of processing time to retrieve a cell value along with its format, and it is for this reason that this property is slow.

.Value

The .Value keyword is a slight improvement over the previous keyword since it does not return a value with its format. Regardless of whether a cell has been formatted with a date or currency, this keyword will only return the VBA date and VBA currency, and the values for these outputs are truncated at decimal places.

.Value2

The .Value2 keyword only returns the underlying value of the cell. This keyword does not take any formatting into account and works faster than the .Text and .Value keywords. This keyword works faster if you use a variant array.

If you want to learn more about how these keywords work, please read the following post: https://fastexcel.wordpress.com/2011/11/30/text-vs-value-vs-value2-slow-text-and-how-to-avoid-it/

Avoid Using Copy and Paste

When you use the macro recorder to record any operations, including copy and paste that you perform in Excel, the code that the recorder writes will use these methods as default operations. It is always a good idea to avoid using the copy and paste operations, and use some in-built VBA functions to perform these operations. You can also use the in-built functions to copy formulae or formatting across a block of cells. The following example will give you an idea about how you should use the in-built VBA operations and functions as opposed to manual copy and paste operations.

Before

>Range("A1").Select
>
>Selection.Copy
>
>Range("A2").Select
>
>ActiveSheet.Paste

After

>' Approach 1: copy everything (formulas, values and formatting
>
>Range("A1").Copy Destination:=Range("A2")
>
>' Approach 2: copy values only
>
>Range("A2").Value2 = Range("A1").Value2
>
>' Approach 3: copy formulas only
>
>Range("A2").Formula = Range("A1").Formula

If you think that the code is still functioning slowly, you can use the following fix: https://support.microsoft.com/en-in/help/2817672/macro-takes-longer-than-expected-to-execute-many-in

Use The Option Explicit Keyword To Catch Undeclared Variables

Option Explicit is one of the many Module directives that you can use in VBA. This directive will instruct VBA about how it should treat a code within a specific module. If you use Option Explicit, you should ensure that all the variables in the code are declared. If there is any variable that is not declared, it will throw a compile error. This will help you catch any variables that have been named incorrectly. It will also help to improve the performance of the macro where variables are defined at different times. You can set this by typing "Option Explicit" at the top of every module you write. Alternatively, you can check the "Require Variable Declaration" in the VBA editor under "Tools -> Options."

Chapter Four

Some Problems with Spreadsheets and How to Overcome Them

Most people use Excel to make a repository. This is because it is easy to make a list of small items for yourself or your colleagues in Excel. You may perhaps want to use some formulae to create something sophisticated. You may also want to use macros to automate the process of collecting and processing data. You can do this by typing an equal to sign in the cell before you write the formula. Excel will be your guide. There are some problems that everybody will face when it comes to using Excel, and that is its simplicity. You may start with a small project in Excel, and this project will grow until it becomes a daunting task. At this point, you may also face some issues with stability and speed, or some development problem that you cannot solve.

This chapter examines some of the common issues that people come across when they use spreadsheets, and also provides some solutions to tackle those problems. It will also tell you when you should switch to a database instead of sticking to Excel.

Multi-User Editing

When an Excel system begins to grow, you will quickly run into a problem where only one user can open the workbook at a time and make changes to it. Any other person who wants to open the workbook will be notified that someone already has the book open and that they can view the workbook as a read-only version or wait until the file is closed by the first user. Excel does promise to let you know when the first user has closed the file, but this is a hollow promise since Excel does not always check the status, and there are times when it may never give you an update. Even if it does give you an update, someone may already have opened the file before you.

You can get around this in the following ways:

- You should use Excel Online. This application is a web-based and abridged version of Microsoft Excel.
- Turn on the feature that will allow you to share the workbook.
- Split the workbook into smaller workbooks. This will allow different users to access different workbooks without causing any hindrances in the work.

Shared Workbooks

If you use Excel online, you can allow multiple users to edit the workbook at the same time. There is so much functionality that goes missing, which makes it a contender only for simple tasks. The shared workbook features in Excel will allow you to share the workbook between multiple users, but there are many restrictions. For instance, you cannot delete a group of cells or create a table in a shared workbook.

It is easy to walk around some restrictions, but for others, it is a matter of changing the structure of the entire workbook instead of using a workbook that has already been set up. These workarounds can, however, get in the way. As a result of this, it is impossible to use a workbook that is shared in the same way that you may use a single user workbook.

Any changes made in a shared workbook will be synchronized between the users every time the workbook is saved. These changes can be saved on a time schedule, meaning that a workbook can be saved or force saved every few minutes. The overhead of regular checking and savings every share user change is quite large. The size of the workbook can increase which will put a strain on your network thereby slowing down every other system.

A shared workbook is prone to corruption. Microsoft office knows that this is the problem, but there is nothing much you can do about the issue. The alternative to this situation is to use Excel online since you can have multiple users working on the same workbook. Not many users will switch to excel online until Microsoft will remove all the restrictions on a shared workbook, and extend a multi-authoring tool to the Excel offline application.

Linked Workbooks

If you want to overcome the issue of multi-user editing, you should try to split the data across multiple workbooks. It is likely that these workbooks must be linked so that any value entered in one can be used in another. The links between workbooks also help to separate data using a logical method instead of using separate worksheets in one workbook.

Unfortunately, these links lead to instability and frustration. This is because the links need to be absolute or relative. In the case of absolute links, you will need to include the full path resource workbook while in the case of relative links, you only need to include the difference between the destination and source paths. This may sound sensible until you come across the rules the Excel decides to employ on when you can use each type of link, and when you can change them.

These rules are governed by numerous options. Some of these rules are dependent on whether the workbook was saved and whether it was saved before every link was inserted. There are times when Excel will automatically change the link when you open a workbook and use the save as option to copy the file. Excel may also change the links when you simply save the workbook down. One of the main disadvantages of using this option is that the links can break easily, and it is difficult to recover all the broken links. This is also a time-consuming affair since you cannot use the files that are affected by the broken links.

The linked data will only be updated when all the underlying files are open unless you edit links and update values. It is because of this that you may need to open 3 or 4 workbooks to ensure that all the information is flowing through in the right order. If you made it changed it the value in the first workbook but open only 3rd workbook, you will not see any changes because this is a second workbook still does not have the updated values.

It is logical to create a change a data, but this will increase the likelihood that the data is incorrect or and when you open a workbook somebody else is already editing the underlying work. You can avoid the use of link workbooks, but there is a chance that you will end up entering the same data in more than one workbook. The danger with this is that you may type the data differently each time.

Data Validation

You must remember that any user can enter data on any computer system. People can transpose digits in numbers or mistype words with monotonous regularity. You must ensure that you check the data when it is entered or you will have a problem in the end.

Excel will always accept whatever any user types. Therefore, it is possible to set up a validation using lists, but it is impossible to maintain this list especially if that field is used in multiple places. For example, if a user should enter a customer reference number or a document ID they can enter the wrong record. To avoid this, it is always good to have some checks across the workbook. If there is no Data integrity, the system will be fatally compromised, which will affect the analysis.

You may already be suffering from this problem without having realized what the root cause is. Let us consider a situation where there is a list of invoices that you have entered in Excel Find the user has typed the name of every customer differently on every invoice. You got invoices to John limited, John Ltd and John. You are aware that these invoices point to the same company or customer, but Excel is not aware of this. This means that any analysis that you made using this data will always give you multiple results when they should only be one.

Navigation Issues

It is difficult to navigate through large workbooks. The number of sheet tabs in the bottom of the window is difficult to use and is a terrible way to find your way around the workbook. If there are many sheets in the workbook, and you cannot see all of them on the screen, it will be difficult for you to find what you are looking for. You can always click on the arrow to the left of your active sheet, but you will only see the first twenty sheets in that window. You cannot sort or group the list of sheets in any order.

Security Issues

You can add a lot of security features to an Excel workbook, but it is still going to have many problems. It is more important to work toward protecting the structure of the workbook, instead of worrying about the data. You can always lock some sheets and cells in the workbook to prevent some users from making any changes to the data or formulae. Regardless of whether you protect the sheet or not, if someone can see the data, they can make changes to it. You can avoid this by using some clever macro skills.

Speed Issues

You must remember that Excel is not the fastest application there is, and the programming language we use in Excel, VBA is slow and slightly sluggish when compared to the more professional languages like C and C#. This is because of the intended use of Excel and its flexibility. You should remember that Excel is a spreadsheet engine alone, and it can only be used to manage large volumes of data. This does not mean that you must always use Excel for this type of work. There are many other applications that you can use to perform such tasks since those applications were designed to perform these functions.

Enter the database

If you are facing any of the issues that have been listed above, you should not ignore them. The answer or solution to these problems is to store the data in a structured manner. This means that we will need to start saving data in a database. This will allow you to think about your data in a logical manner. You have the ability to see how the data welding together and how you will need to interact with it to analyze the information.

You must, however, take heed. If you move from spreadsheets to databases, you should not duplicate the design of a spreadsheet. Instead, you should find a way to make the design better. There are some general database applications, listed below with which you can construct a simple solution. Alternatively, you can also use specialist database applications that allow you to switch from spreadsheet to databases within a few minutes point these applications are a better fit to big data.

For example, if you have a list of customers, their details and any interaction you have had with these customers you should consider using a customer relationship management system. Customer relationship management system is a specialized database. Similarly, you can save accounts on packages like Sage and QuickBooks. The may be times when you cannot find an existing application to suit your needs. As such times you may need to build a database by yourself or request see IT department or any consultant to build the database for you.

The relational database is the most common type of database used in today's world. This database stores information or data in the form of tables, which consists of columns and rows of data. Every row data will hold a separate item and every column will describe a different attribute of that item. For example, if the rows hold customer information, the columns can describe attributes like customer name and customer ID. All you need to do is enter the data once, and then you can use the same data to print on every invoice.

Every table in a relational database has a relationship between them. You can take the relationship between an invoice and the customer ID. Here you can always find an invoice that is related to a specific customer using the customer ID. Alternatively, you can also retrieve customer information from the invoice if necessary. All you need to do is enter the customer data of one in the database to create a record, and you can use that information across different invoices without having to type the data again. To use or create a database, you must define the tables and the relationships between those tables, and then define the type of layout you want to use to edit or list the data.

There are over a dozen applications that you can choose from. Some of the applications are easy to use and do the job for you. These applications will allow you to define the table, the data screen, and the reports. There are other applications that are more useful in specific areas but will require other tools to perform the job.

For example, some applications may be very powerful when comes defining a table and the relationship that table shares with the database and other tables, and it may also have some excellent analysis and reporting features. This application can, however, lack a tool, which will allow you to define the data entry screen. An obvious example of such an application is Microsoft SQL. As is the case with large database systems, the SQL server will only take care of the back-end annual expect you to use, and other tools like visual studio to develop or maintain the front-end.

Choosing the Right Database

Access

Microsoft Access is one of the oldest databases available. This is easy to use and is extremely easy to abuse. You can design screens, reports, and tables from scratch or use an existing template. Some of the templates in Access do not teach you some good practices, but they will help you get started quickly. The programming and screen features and options are sophisticated, and you can deploy the application on the intranet without having to rely on sharing the files with users.

SharePoint

SharePoint is a document storage application and a database. This application can be used to compile and link simple lists. You can use the form designer to customize your dashboard, but it is important to remember that it is not a sophisticated application to use. SharePoint has the ability to suck the information from Excel and put it into a custom list. This makes it a useful application since everybody in your network will have access to the list. You can choose to add some security features, which will restrict the access for some people. SharePoint can also send you an alert email when someone makes a change – adds, deletes or edits – to a record. You can also synchronize the information with Outlook if you have some data that concerns a person, calendar or task.

Zoho Creator

There is a database application that you can use in the Zoho office services available on the internet. You can drag and drop the required layout in an easy way. This will also help you decide how the work should flow and what the interaction can be like. Since this is a web application, the data you use and the applications you develop can be found anywhere. Therefore, you should use the simple security features that this application provides to keep your data private. Zoho charges you per month but will allow you to store only some records depending on the price you choose to pay. If you want to use advanced features like email integration, you will need to pay an additional amount of money.

Hi there! If you found the topic or information useful, it would be a great help if you can leave a quick review on Amazon. Thanks a lot!

Chapter Five

Sub Procedures

If you have read Excel tutorials that talk about VBA and macros, you would have come across the term procedure at least a hundred times. If you are unsure of what these are, you should learn this now. There are many good reasons why this is important.

If you want to become an expert at writing macros and using VBA, you should understand what a procedure is, the different types of procedures and how you should work with them. This is one of the most essential tools to learn if you want to become a VBA expert. This chapter will provide all the information you need about procedures and will dig deeper into the concepts of sub procedures. Let us first begin with an introduction to sub procedures.

What Is A Sub Procedure?

If you have written programs or code in VBA, you will know that a procedure is a block of code or statements that are enclosed between a declaration statement and an End statement. The purpose of the procedure is to perform a specific action or task. All the instructions that you want to give the compiler are within a procedure. If you want to master coding in VBA, you should fully understand this concept. There are two types of procedures in VBA – Function procedures and sub procedures. This chapter will focus only on Sub procedures.

The following are the differences between a VBA sub procedure and a function procedure:

- A VBA sub procedure will perform some function or action with Excel. This means that when you execute a sub procedure, Excel will do something. The changes or functions that happen in Excel depend on what the code says.

- A function procedure will perform some calculations and return a value. The value returned can either be an array, number or string. If you have worked regularly with functions in Excel, you already know how the function procedure will work. This is because they work in the same way as Excel functions. These procedures will perform some function on the data in Excel and return a value.

Experts say that most macros that people write are sub procedures. If you always use the macro recorder to create your macro, you are creating a sub procedure. From the above comments, it is clear that you will work a lot with Excel VBA Sub procedures.

How Does The VBA Sub Procedure Look?

The image below will show you how a VBA sub procedure looks. You should notice that this procedure has the following features:

- It begins with the statement "Sub." This is the declaration statement.

- There is an End declaration statement.

- There is a block of code that is enclosed between the declaration statements.

```
Sub Delete_Blank_Rows_3()
'
' Delete_Blank_Rows_3 Macro
' Deletes rows when cells within the row are blank.
'
' Keyboard Shortcut: Ctrl+Shift+B
'

    On Error Resume Next
    Selection.EntireRow.SpecialCells(xlBlanks).EntireRow.Delete
    On Error GoTo 0

End Sub
```

(https://powerspreadsheets.com/vba-sub-procedures/)

The purpose of this VBA sub procedure is to delete some rows in the worksheet where there are blank cells. Before we move on, let us take a look at the first statement in the sub procedure. There are three sections to look at:

- The sub keyword, also the declaration statement, which tells the compiler that the sub procedure has started.

- The name of the sub procedure. We will cover the rules that must be followed when working with sub procedures in the following sections.

- The parentheses in the sub procedure are where you will need to add the arguments that you will be using from other procedures. You should separate these by using a comma. You can always create a VBA sub procedure that does not use any arguments. You should, however, include an empty set of parentheses when you name the sub procedure.

The following are the four elements that you should include in a VBA sub procedure:

- Sub statement

- Name

- Parentheses
- End Sub keyword

You can include two optional elements in a sub procedure:

- A list of arguments that you will need to include in the parentheses.
- Valid instructions that are included in the declaration statements in the code.

Apart from these, you can include three optional items in a VBA sub procedure. These items are optional, but they are important to consider. Before we look at them, let us look at how this procedure will be structured.

[Private/Public] [Static] Sub name ([Argument list])

[Instructions]

[Exit Sub]

[Instructions]

End Sub

To learn more about the Sub statement, you should read the articles found in the Microsoft Dev Center. Let us take a look at the optional elements that are present in the above structure. These items are written in square brackets to indicate that they are optional.

Element #1: [Private/Public]

The keywords private and public are called access modifiers. If you type private before the declaration statement in a sub procedure, it implies that only the procedures or codes written within the same module can access that sub procedure.

If you choose to use the keyword public, the sub procedure will not have any access restrictions. Despite this, if you were to use the keywords option private statement at the beginning of the sub procedure, any procedure outside the relevant project cannot refer to or use the sub procedure. We will talk a little more about the scope of the project in the sections below.

Element #2: [Static]

If you use the keyword static at the beginning of the sub procedure, any variable, which is the part of the sub procedure will be preserved even when the module ends.

Element #3: [Exit Sub]

The exit sub statement is the final declaration statement, which is used to immediately exit A sub procedure. This means that any statements within the sub procedure not run once the compiler reaches this decoration statement.

How to Name A VBA Sub Procedure

You must always name a procedure. The rules that you need to follow when naming A sub procedure are given below:

- You should always use a letter as the first character.

- The remaining characters in the name can be numbers, letters or some punctuation characters. For example, the following characters can't be used: #, $, %, &, @, ^, * and !

- You should avoid using spaces and periods.

- Since VBA is not a case sensitive language, cannot distinguish between lowercase and uppercase letters.

- Any sub procedure can have a name, which has a maximum of 255 characters.

Experts suggest that we be a procedure name should always:

- Describe what the purpose of the sub procedure is or what it is supposed to do.

- Have some meaning.

- Be a combination of a noun and a verb.

There are some programmers who choose useful sentences to name the sub procedures. There is one advantage and disadvantage of doing this:

- A sentence will definitely let any other user of programmer know what the purpose of the sub procedure is. This is because a sentence is very unambiguous and descriptive.

- When you type of full sentence you will use more time. This means that you will take longer to finish your macro.

I believe that you should always use a name that is descriptive, unambiguous and meaningful. It is at this point that you should choose what your style is, and always stick to something that is comfortable and will help you achieve your goals.

How to Determine the Scope of A VBA Sub Procedure

The scope will define how you are when you should call upon a VBA sub procedure. When you create a BBA procedure you have the option to determine which other procedure can call it. You can do this by using the keywords public and private which were introduced in the above section as an optional element of a procedure.

Let us now take a look at what the meaning of these keywords is and how you can determine whether a specific VBA procedure is public or private.

Public VBA Sub Procedures

Every sub procedure is public by default. If a specific procedure is public there is no access restriction. Since the default option is that a procedure is public, you do not have to include the public keyword at the beginning of the name. For instance, the following procedure delete_blank_rows_3 is a public procedure although we did not use the keyword public.

```
Sub Delete_Blank_Rows_3()

    ' Delete_Blank_Rows_3 Macro
    ' Delete rows when cells within the row are blank.
    '
    ' Keyboard Shortcut: Ctrl+Shift+B
    '

    On Error Resume Next
    Selection.EntireRow.SpecialCells(xlBlanks).EntireRow.Delete
    On Error GoTo 0

End Sub
```

no "Public"

(https://powerspreadsheets.com/vba-sub-procedures/)

If you want to make the courts near, you should try to include the public keyword in the procedure. Most programmers do follow this practice. In the image below, you will see that the keyword public has been included in the delete_blank_rows_3 macro.

```
Public Sub Delete_Blank_Rows_3()
'
' Delete_Blank_Rows_3 Macro
' Deletes rows when cells within the row are blank.
'
' Keyboard Shortcut: Ctrl+Shift+B
'

On Error Resume Next
Selection.EntireRow.SpecialCells(xlBlanks).EntireRow.Delete
On Error GoTo 0

End Sub
```

(https://powerspreadsheets.com/vba-sub-procedures/)

In both cases, the sub procedure is public. In simple words both the macros, with and without the public keyword are the same.

Private VBA Sub Procedures

When you use the private keyword ahead of the sub procedure, the content of the statements within the sub procedure can only be accessed by other procedures within the same module. If there is any other procedure or module that wants to access this sir procedure it cannot, even if the module is in the same Excel workbook. For instance, if you need the delete_blank_rows_3 macro a private macro you will need to follow the syntax given in the image below.

```
Private Sub Delete_Blank_Rows_3()
'
' Delete_Blank_Rows_3 Macro
' Deletes rows when cells within the row are blank.
'
' Keyboard Shortcut: Ctrl+Shift+B
'

On Error Resume Next
Selection.EntireRow.SpecialCells(xlBlanks).EntireRow.Delete
On Error GoTo 0

End Sub
```

(https://powerspreadsheets.com/vba-sub-procedures/)

How to Make All VBA Sub Procedures in a Module Private to A VBA Project

A person using the public in the private keywords, you can also make a sub procedure accessible to other modules in different BBA project by using the option private statement. To use the option private statement, you must include the keywords "option private module" before the sub procedure. If you are certain that you want to use this statement ensure that the keywords are ahead of the declaration statement in the sub procedure.

The image below shows how VBA uses three different methods to delete a row based on whether the row has an empty cell or not. The third macro or sub procedure in the image below is the Delete_Blank_Rows_3 macro. This macro does not appear fully in the image.

Found this title interesting or useful? Then a review on Amazon will be highly appreciated!

```
Option Private Module

Sub Delete_Blank_Rows()

'
' Delete_Blank_Rows Macro
' Deletes rows with blank cells in selected range.
'
' Keyboard Shortcut: Ctrl+Shift+D
'
    On Error Resume Next
        Range("E6:E257").Select
        Selection.SpecialCells(xlCellTypeBlanks).EntireRow.Delete
End Sub
Sub Delete_Blank_Rows_2()

'
' Delete_Blank_Rows_2 Macro
' Deletes rows with blank cells in selected range.
'
' Keyboard Shortcut: Ctrl+Shift+E
'
    On Error Resume Next
    With Range("E6:E257")
        .Value = .Value
        .SpecialCells(xlCellTypeBlanks).EntireRow.Delete
    End With

End Sub
Sub Delete_Blank_Rows_3()

'
' Delete_Blank_Rows_3 Macro
' Deletes rows when cells within the row are blank
```

(https://powerspreadsheets.com/vba-sub-procedures/)

All the sub procedure is in the above image can only be accessed referenced by module or the procedures in the VBA project that contains them.

When to Make VBA Sub Procedures Private: An Example

You can always execute A sub procedure by using another procedure to call it. Most programmers use this method to run or execute a procedure. In some cases, you may also have procedures that are designed to be called by other sub procedures. If you have any procedures in a specific workbook, it is always good to make them private. When you do this the sub procedure will no longer be listed in the macro dialog box. The macro dialog box is one of the easiest and fastest ways to execute A sub procedure.

If you do not understand how this works, do not worry. I will explain how you can call VBA sub procedure from other procedure or by using the macro dialogue box in the section below.

How to Execute / Run / Call a VBA Sub Procedure

When you work with macros you will often use the terms run execute or call interchangeably. These words refer to the action of executing the statements in the sub procedure. You can use these words interchangeably.

You can execute run a call A sub procedure in many ways. This section provides 9 different ways in which you can execute or run the statements in a procedure. There is a 10th option, which you can use but this is out of the scope of this book. This in this option you will need to execute the macro or the statement using a customized context menu. This section does not talk about using a context menu customization to run a block of code since it is a separate topic that we need to be covered extensively.

We will use the delete_blank_rows_3 macro as an example in all the options in this section.

Option One: How to Execute A VBA Sub Procedure Directly From the Visual Basic Editor

Experts state that this is the best and the fastest way to execute the block of code in a sub procedure. In this method, you will run the procedure directly in the visual basic editor using the module in which it is written.

Describe the factor this is one of the fastest methods, most people do not use it often. In practice, people often execute the macro only when they are in excel and not in the visual basic editor. There are some other options that are listed in this section, which will allow you to do this.

This method will only work when a specific sub procedure that you want to run does not require any arguments from other procedures and macros. The reason is that this option does not allow you to use any arguments are inputs from other procedures.

If you ever want to run a sub procedure, which contains arguments, you can only do it by calling it from another procedure. The procedure used to call the sub procedure will need to pass the arguments that the sub procedure required to execute the block of code.

If you do choose to use this method to call or run the code in the sub procedure, you should follow the following steps:

Step One: Open the Visual Basic Editor

You can open the visual basic editor using the keyboard shortcut Alt + F11. Alternatively, you can go to the developer tab in the ribbon and choose the visual basic icon.

(https://powerspreadsheets.com/vba-sub-procedures/)

Step Two: Open The VBA Module That Contains The VBA Sub Procedure You Want To Execute.

You now want the visual basic editor to give you the code that is in the sub procedure that you are calling. This can be done in several ways. One of the easiest methods is to double click on the relevant module or procedure. For instance, if the sub procedure that you want to call is within module 1, you will simply need to click module 1 in the project explorer in the visual basic editor.

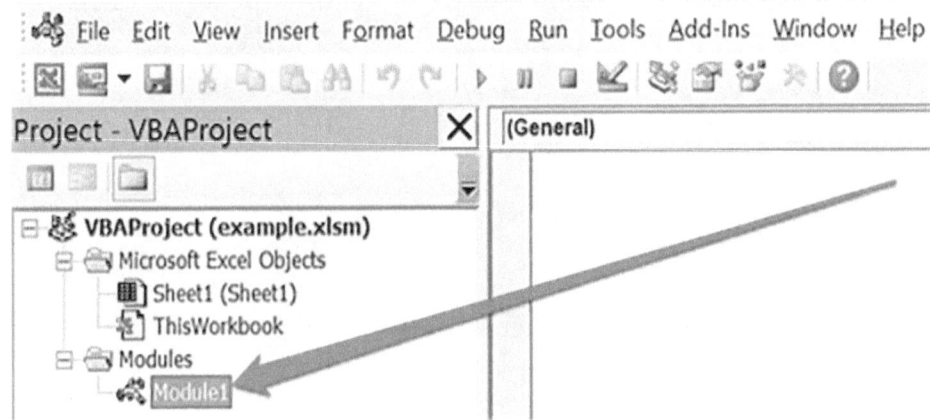

(https://powerspreadsheets.com/vba-sub-procedures/)

As a result of this, the visual basic editor will display the relevant code in the programming window in the visual basic environment.

```
Sub Delete_Blank_Rows_3()

' Delete_Blank_Rows_3 Macro
' Deletes rows when cells within the row are blank.
'
' Keyboard Shortcut: Ctrl+Shift+B
'
    On Error Resume Next
    Selection.EntireRow.SpecialCells(xlBlanks).EntireRow.Delete
    On Error GoTo 0

End Sub
```

(https://powerspreadsheets.com/vba-sub-procedures/)

Step Three: Run The VBA Sub Procedure.

If you want to call A sub procedure directly using the relevant module in the visual basic editor, you must use the following methods:

- Go to the run menu and click on the option "Run Sub/UserForm."

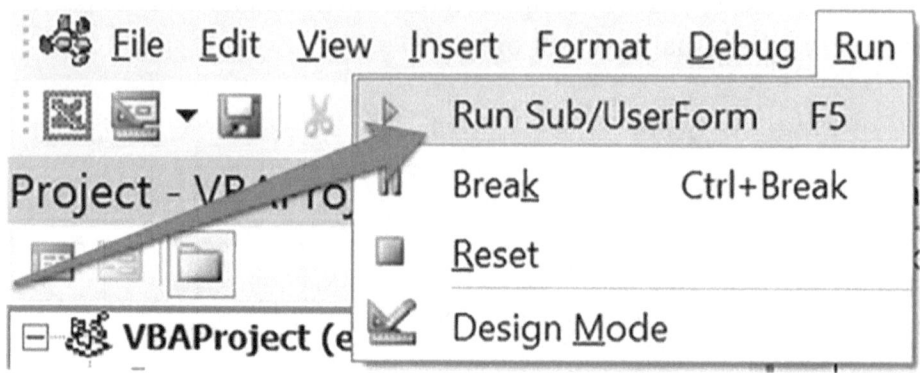

(https://powerspreadsheets.com/vba-sub-procedures/)

- Click on F5, which is the keyboard shortcut.

Option Two: How to Execute A VBA Sub Procedure Using the Macro Dialog

This method, as the first method, will only work when the sub procedure does not require any arguments. It is because of the same reason mentioned earlier - you cannot specify the arguments.

Regardless of what the arguments are, this is an option that most programmers used to execute sub procedures. When you use this method you can run the sub procedure in two steps. Let us look at them.

Step One: Open the Macro dialog.

You should first instruct Excel to open the macro dialog box using the following methods:

- Click on Alt + F8, which is the shortcut key.
- Go to the developer tab in the ribbon, and click on the macros option.

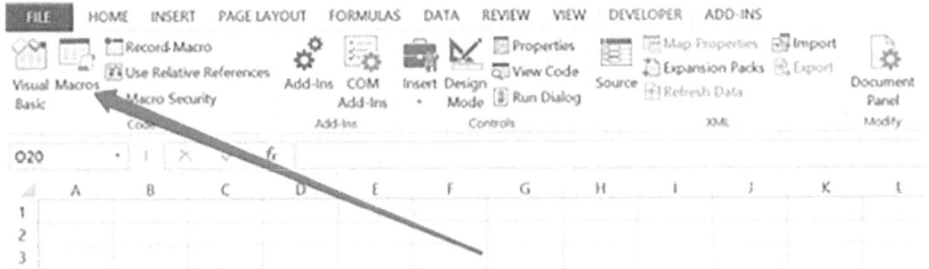

(https://powerspreadsheets.com/vba-sub-procedures/)

Excel window display the macro dialog box which will look as follows:

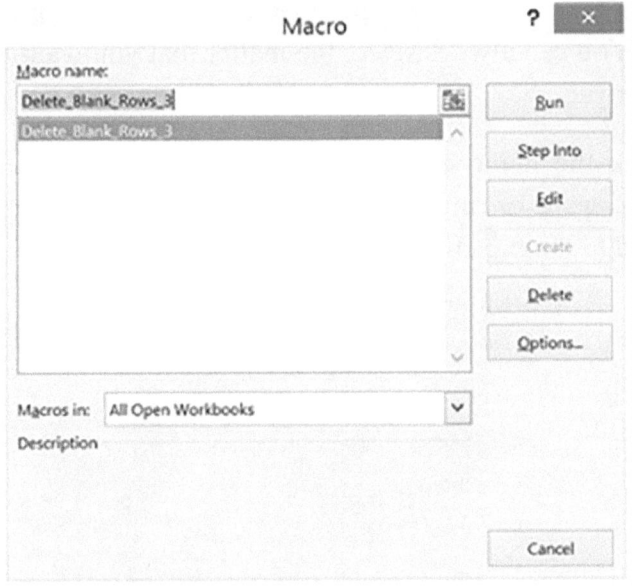

(https://powerspreadsheets.com/vba-sub-procedures/)

Step Two: Select The Macro You Want To Execute And Execute It.

In the above image, you will notice that there is only one macro open in every Excel workbook. This macro is the Delete_Blank_Rows_3 macro. Since this is the only method that is listed, we will only be running or executing the code within that macro.

You are already aware that when you use this method you cannot use any arguments in the sub procedure. Therefore any sab procedure that requires arguments will not appear in the macro dialog box.

It is also important to remember that the macro dialog box will only show procedures that are public. You can still execute A sub procedure, which is private. For this, you should fill the relevant sub procedure name in the macro name field, which appears in the image below. The macro dialogue box does not show any sub procedure, which contains and adding. In this case, you can execute a macro by typing in the relevant macro in the name field.

The rule to select and run or execute macro is the same regardless of whether you have one or multiple macros in the open or active Excel workbook. You can always select the matter that you want to run in the following ways:

Double click the name of the matter that you want to execute. For example, we want to run the Delete_Blank_Rows_3 macro. For this, we will need to double click on the name of the macro.

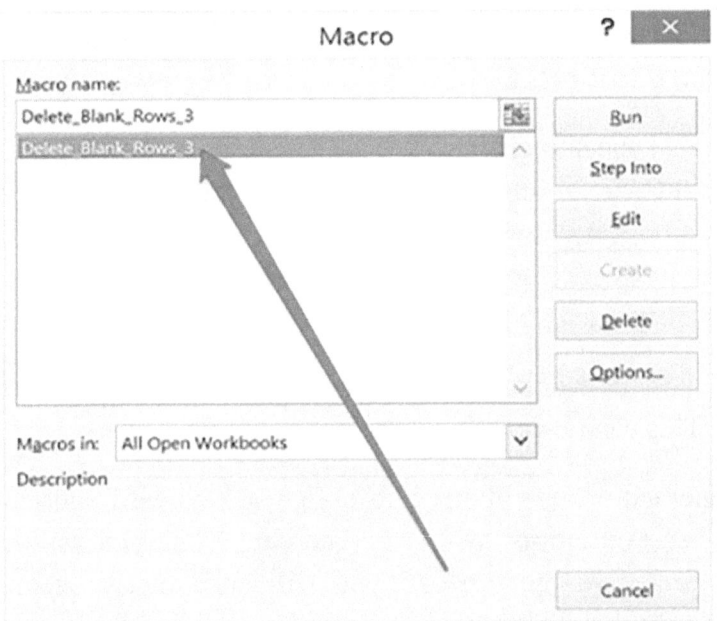

(https://powerspreadsheets.com/vba-sub-procedures/)

Click on the name of the macro you want to run, and hit run button on the top right corner.

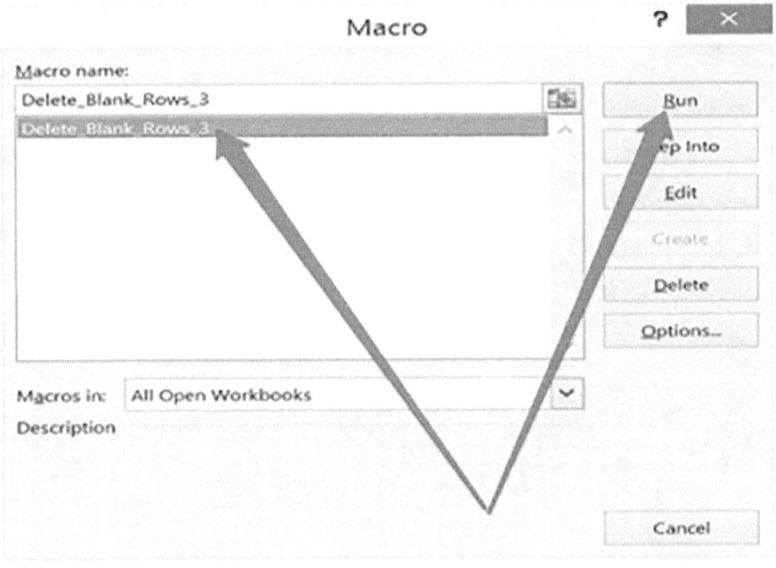

(https://powerspreadsheets.com/vba-sub-procedures/)

Option Three: How to Execute A VBA Sub Procedure Using a Keyboard Shortcut

You can also execute or run a sub procedure using keyboard shortcuts. If you want to run a sub procedure using this method you have to select a press the relevant key combination. It is important to remember that this does not work for macros that require arguments for the same reason as mentioned above.

You may now be wondering how you can assign keyboard shortcuts to a macro. This can be done in two ways:

In this method, you will need to assign a keyboard shortcut to the macro when you are in the macro recorder. When you use the macro recorder to record the process, you will encounter a record macro dialog box. In this dialog box, you can determine whether you want to call a macro using a keyboard shortcut and also determine which keys will compose that shortcut.

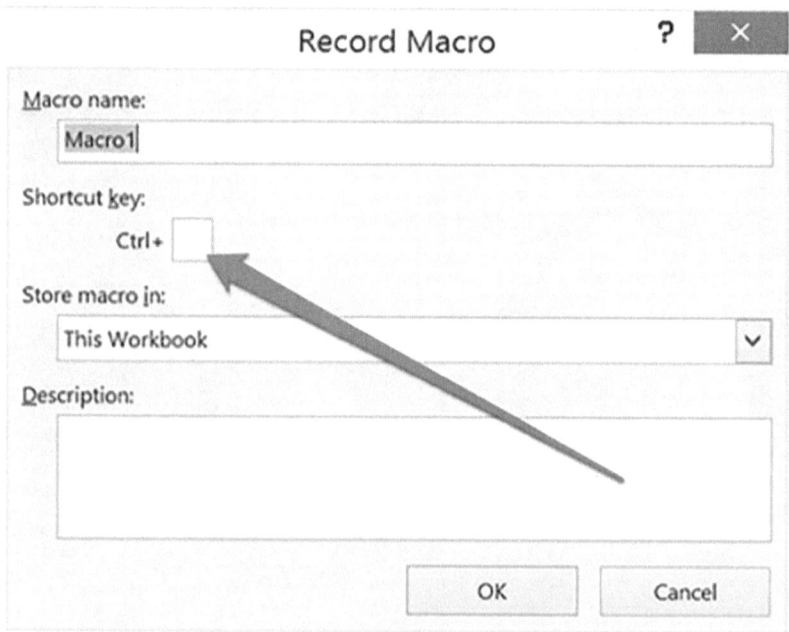

(https://powerspreadsheets.com/vba-sub-procedures/)

This method is more interesting when compared to the previous method. In this method you can assign or edit a keyboard shortcut to any macro in the following method:

Step One: Open The Macro Dialog.

You can use the shortcut Alt + F8 to access the microbe dialogue box. Alternatively, you can go to the developer tab in the ribbon and click on the icon of the macro.

(https://powerspreadsheets.com/vba-sub-procedures/)

Step Two: Select The Macro You Want To Assign A Keyboard Shortcut To.

Now you should select the sub procedure you want to assign a macro to all shortcuts to and click on the options button on the bottom right corner of the dialog box. For example, we have selected the Delete_Blank_Rows_3 macro in the image below.

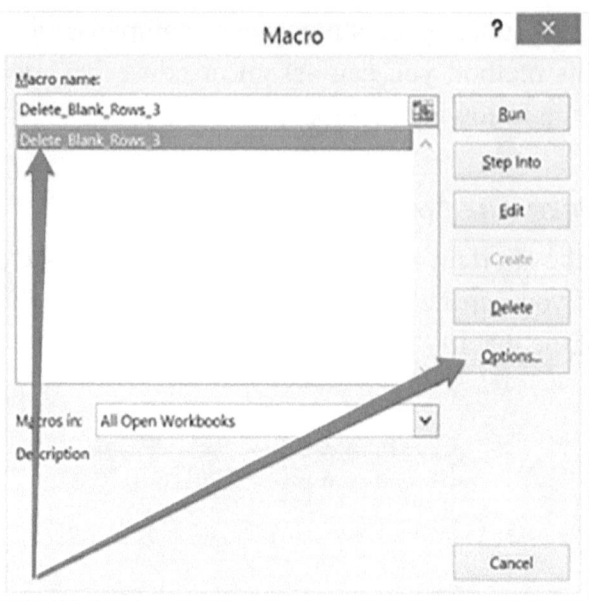

(https://powerspreadsheets.com/vba-sub-procedures/)

Step Three: Assign A Keyboard Shortcut.

When you see the macro option dialog box open, you can assign a keyboard shortcut and click the ok button at the bottom of the box.

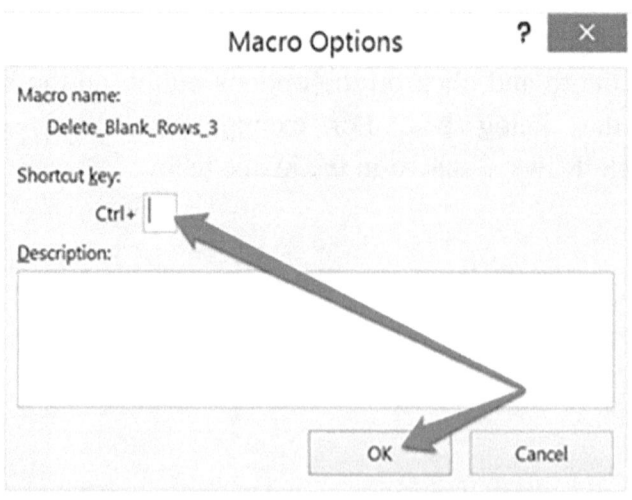

(https://powerspreadsheets.com/vba-sub-procedures/)

It is important to remember that keyboard shortcuts will always take the form of control + letter or control + shift + letter.

When you select the keyboard shortcut, you have to be careful that you are not assigning a combination all shortcuts that already exist in VBA. If you choose as an existing of built-in shortcut, you will be disabling the latter.

For instance, the control + B shortcut is a built-in shortcut for bold. If you assign the same shortcuts to any other Microsoft procedure, you cannot use it to make text bold.

It is always a better idea to use the control + shift + letter form of a shortcut since it reduces the risk of disabling a pre-existing shortcut. Regardless of what the situation is, you have to be careful about what combination you assign a sub procedure.

Option Four: How to Execute A VBA Sub Procedure Using a Button or Other Object

The idea behind using this method is that you can always attach a macro to a specific object. Here I am not referring to a specific object in the macro, but I am referring to the type of object that Excel will allow you to use in a worksheet. Experts have classified these objects into the following classes:

- ActiveX controls
- Form controls
- Inserted objects, like as shapes, text boxes, clip art, SmartArt, WordArt, charts and pictures.

In this section, we will see how you can attach a macro to a button using the form controls option or to any other inserted object in the workbook.

How to Assign a Macro to a Form Control Button

You can attach any macro sub procedure to a form control button using the following four steps:

Step One: Insert a Button

You should first go to the ribbon and navigate to the developer tab. now move to the insert and choose the button form of control. The image below will show you exactly what needs to be done in the step.

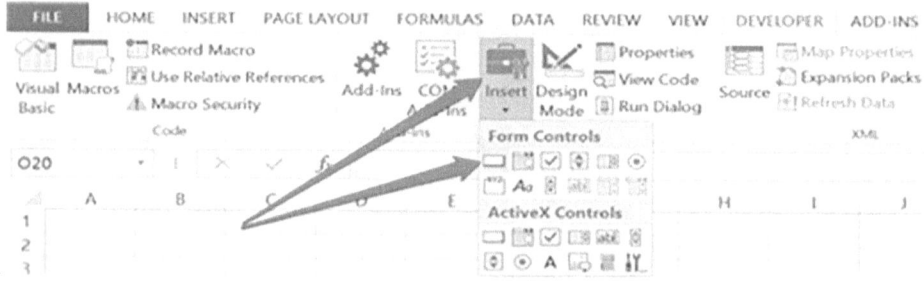

(https://powerspreadsheets.com/vba-sub-procedures/)

Step Two: Create the Button

Now that you have created the button form control, you will need to create the button in the Excel worksheet point you can create the Spartan of places button in any section of the worksheet where you want it to appear.

For example, if I want the button to be in Cell B5, I will click on the top left corner of that cell.

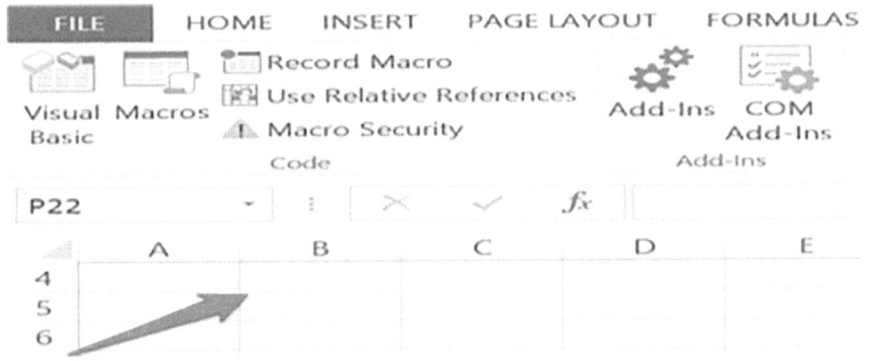

(https://powerspreadsheets.com/vba-sub-procedures/)

Step Three: *Assign a Macro to the Button*

Once you have selected the location where you want the button to be, Excel will display the assign macro dialog box.

(https://powerspreadsheets.com/vba-sub-procedures/)

Based on what the buttons name is, excel will suggest a macro that you can assign to that button. In the example below, we have named the button "Button1_Click."

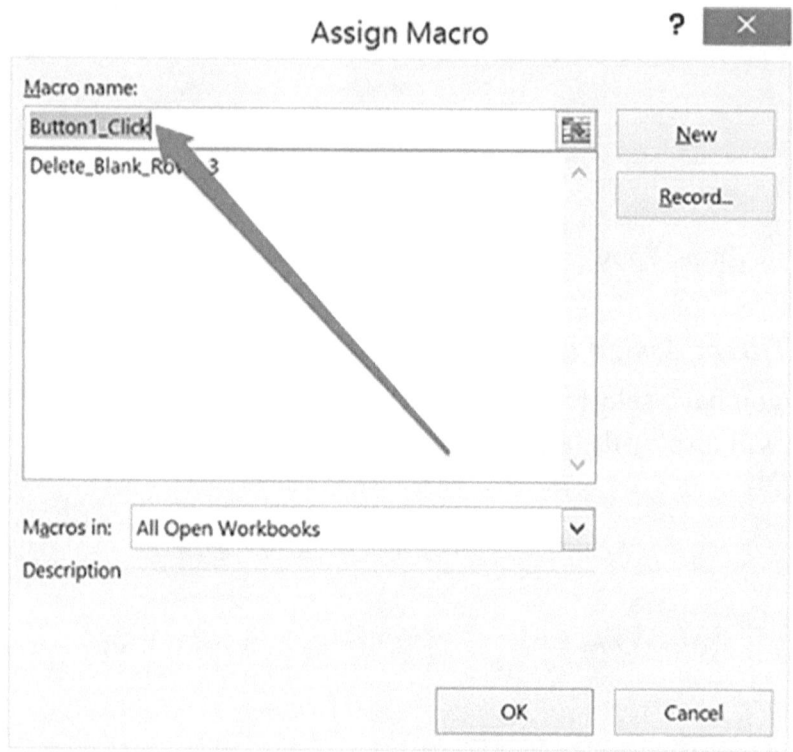

(https://powerspreadsheets.com/vba-sub-procedures/)

In most cases, the suggestion excel gives will not match what you want. Therefore, you have to select a method that you want to assign to the button and then click on ok at the bottom right corner of the dialog box. In the example below, we will be using the Delete_Blank_Rows_3 macro and assign a button to that macro.

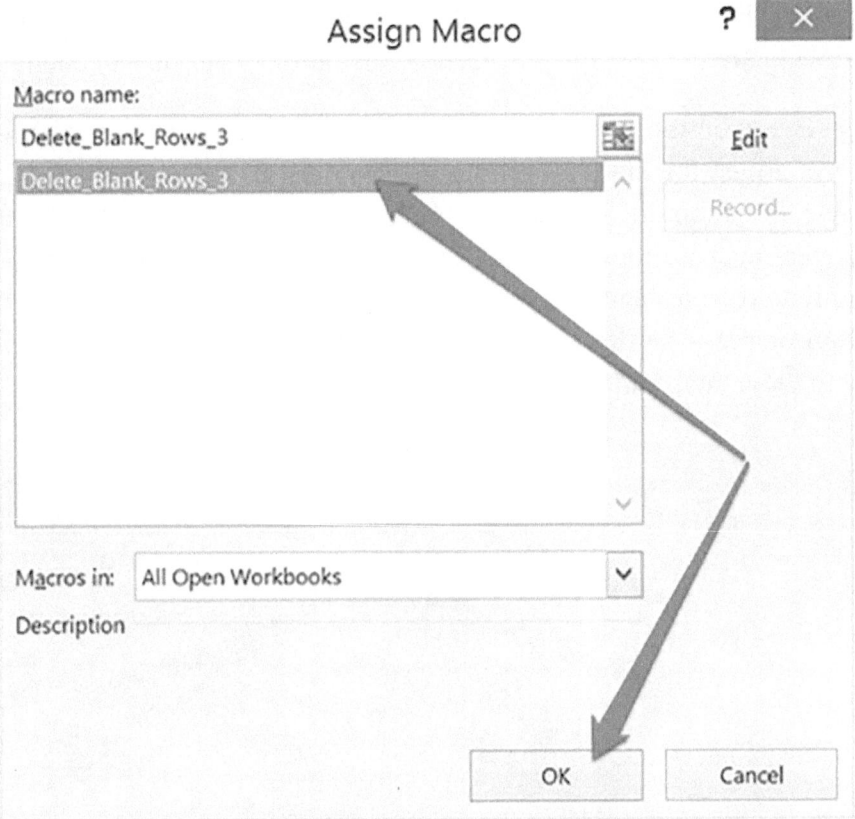

(https://powerspreadsheets.com/vba-sub-procedures/)

Step Four: Edit Button (Optional)

When you have completed the steps described above, Excel will create the button. Now, you only need to execute the relevant sub procedure by clicking on that button.

(https://powerspreadsheets.com/vba-sub-procedures/)

Once the button is in place, you can edit it in some ways. You the following are the four main aspects of the button that you can change:

<u>Size</u>: Every button that you create an Excel has a default size. You can always adjust the size by joining the handles of the button with your mouse. For example, if you want to increase the size of a button so that it covers at least four cells, you can drag the bottom right handle as required. If you cannot find the handles, you can right click on the button or press the left mouse button at the same time as the control key to view the handles.

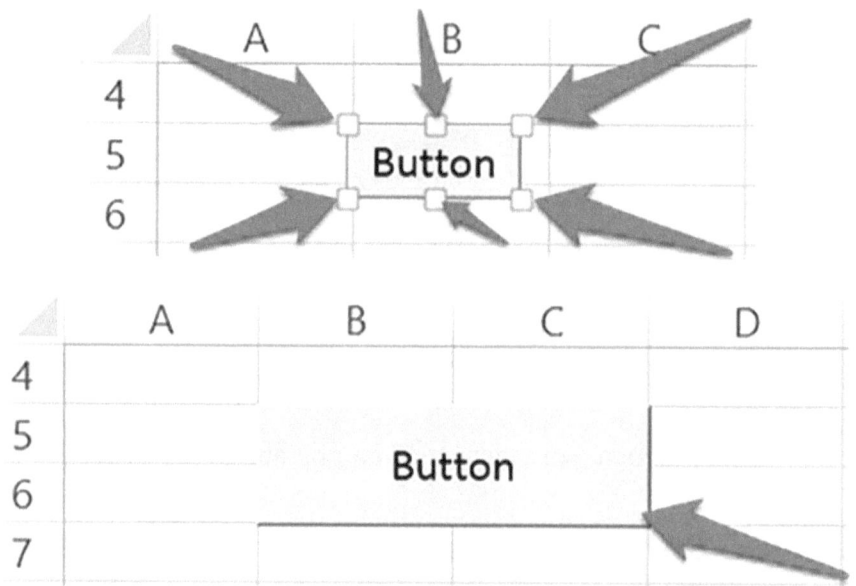

(https://powerspreadsheets.com/vba-sub-procedures/)

<u>Location</u>: You can always modify the location of a button by dragging it with your mouth. You can only track the button using the left button of your mouth is the handles are visible. If they are not visible, you will need to right click on the button and then attempt to drag it to a different location. Alternatively, you can simply change the position of the button by dragging it using the right mouse button. For example, if you want to move the button to cover a couple of cells down, that is it should cover the cells B8, B9, C8 and C9, you should drag the button

until the desired point. When you drive the button excel will show you a Shadow in the new location but will leave the button and its original spot. When you let go or remove your hand from the right now button, accessories display the contextual menu. You should choose the option to move the button by selecting "move here."

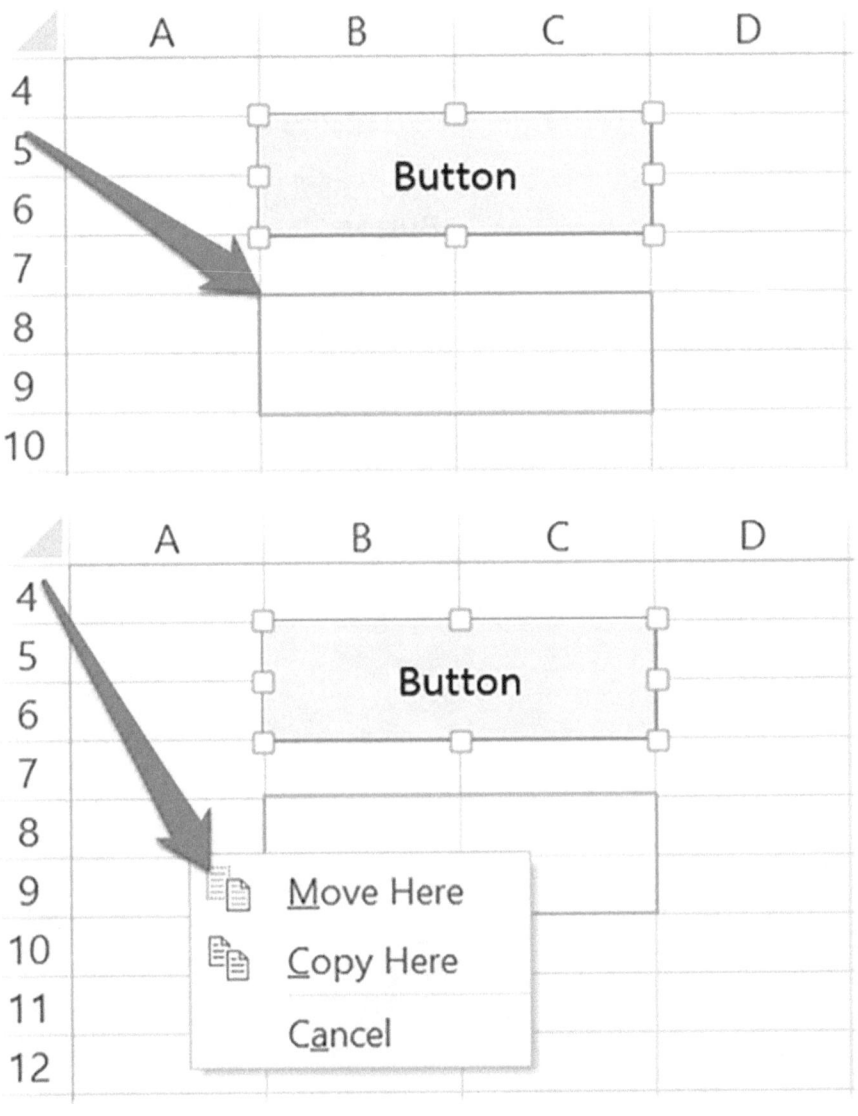

(https://powerspreadsheets.com/vba-sub-procedures/)

Text: If you want to edit the text on the button, you should I click on the button. Excel will then display a contextual menu where you can choose to edit text. Excel word and place the cursor inside the button, so you can modify the text. When you are done click outside of the button to confirm the changes made. Since we are using the Delete_Blank_Rows_3 macro as an example, we will rename the button to delete blank rows in that is more appropriate.

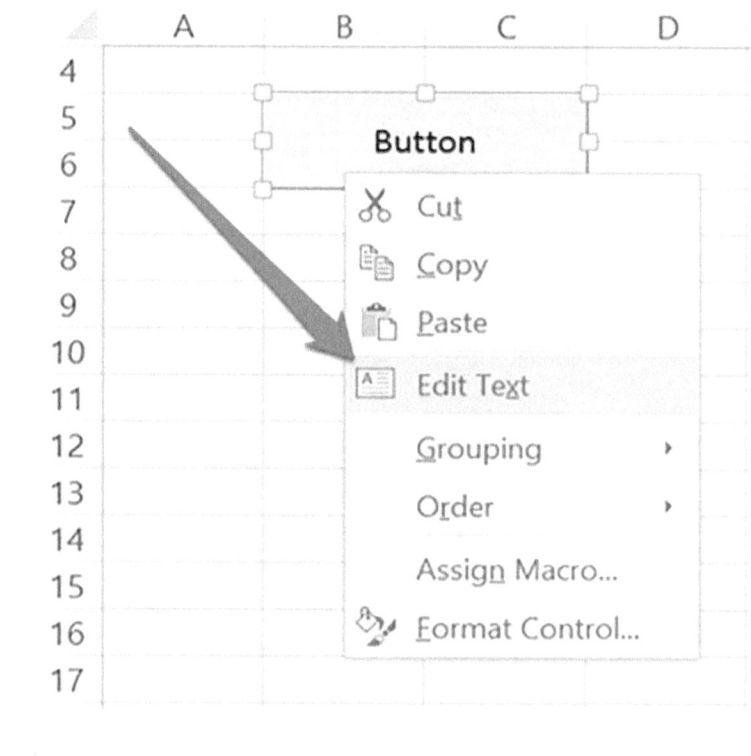

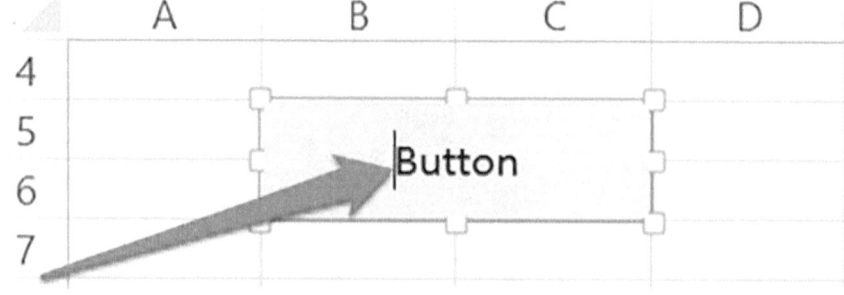

	A	B	C	D
4				
5		Delete Blank Rows		
6				
7				

(https://powerspreadsheets.com/vba-sub-procedures/)

Assigned macro: If there is a necessity, you can always change the VBA sub procedure, and assign it to a different macro by right-clicking on the button. In this case, Excel will take you back to the macro dialogue box where you can select which sub procedure you want to assign to the button. You are already familiar with this process since it has been described above. In addition to this, you can also edit many other aspects of the button by right-clicking on the button and choosing the option to format control. Excel will now display the format control dialogue box. By using the options in this box, you can determine or make changes to many settings of the macro button.

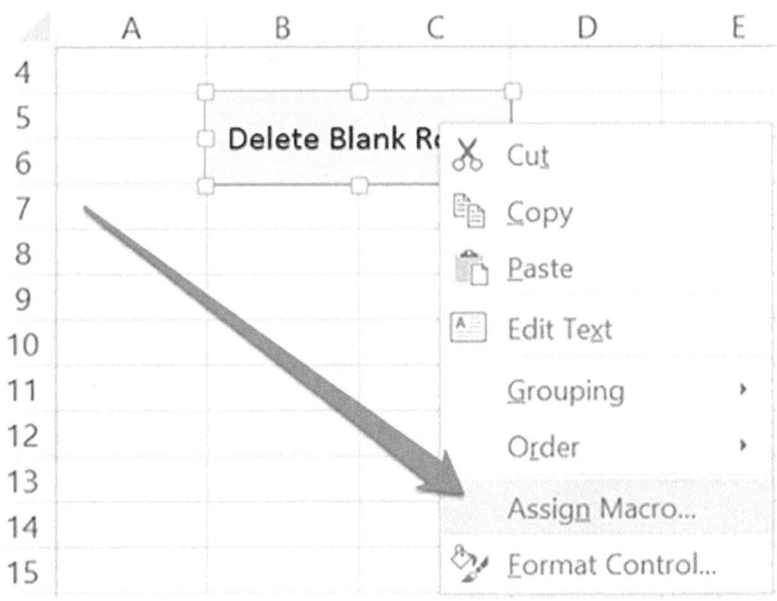

(https://powerspreadsheets.com/vba-sub-procedures/)

Some of the settings that you can change during the format control dialog box are:

- Font, including typeface, style, size, underline, color and effects

- Text alignment and orientation
- Internal margins
- Size
- Whether the button moves and/or sizes with cells

How to Assign a Macro to another Object

In addition to assigning macros to form control buttons, x I will also allow you to assign a macro to other objects. As explain the bug these objects can include text boxes, shapes, SmartArt, WordArt, text boxes, pictures or charts. It is extremely easy to attach a sub procedure to an object in excel. Let us see how you can do this in the case of a word art object which reads delete blank rows.

Step One: Open the Assign Macro Dialog

Right click on the object, and select the assign macro option. This will open the assigned macro dialog box.

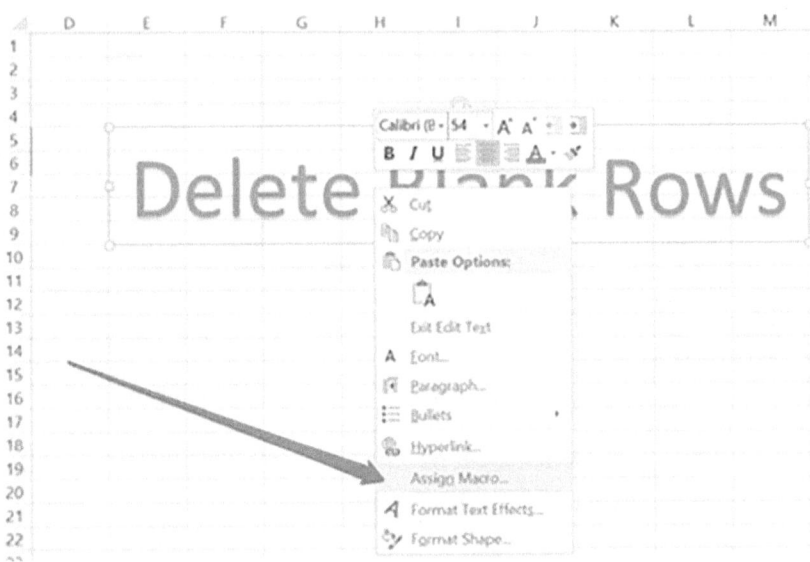

(https://powerspreadsheets.com/vba-sub-procedures/)

Step Two: Select Macro to Assign

Once you complete the step above, Excel will display the macro dialogue box. You are already familiar with this box. To assign a sub procedure to the object in the image above, you should select the matter you want to assign and click ok. In the example below, we will be using the Delete_Blank_Rows_3 macro.

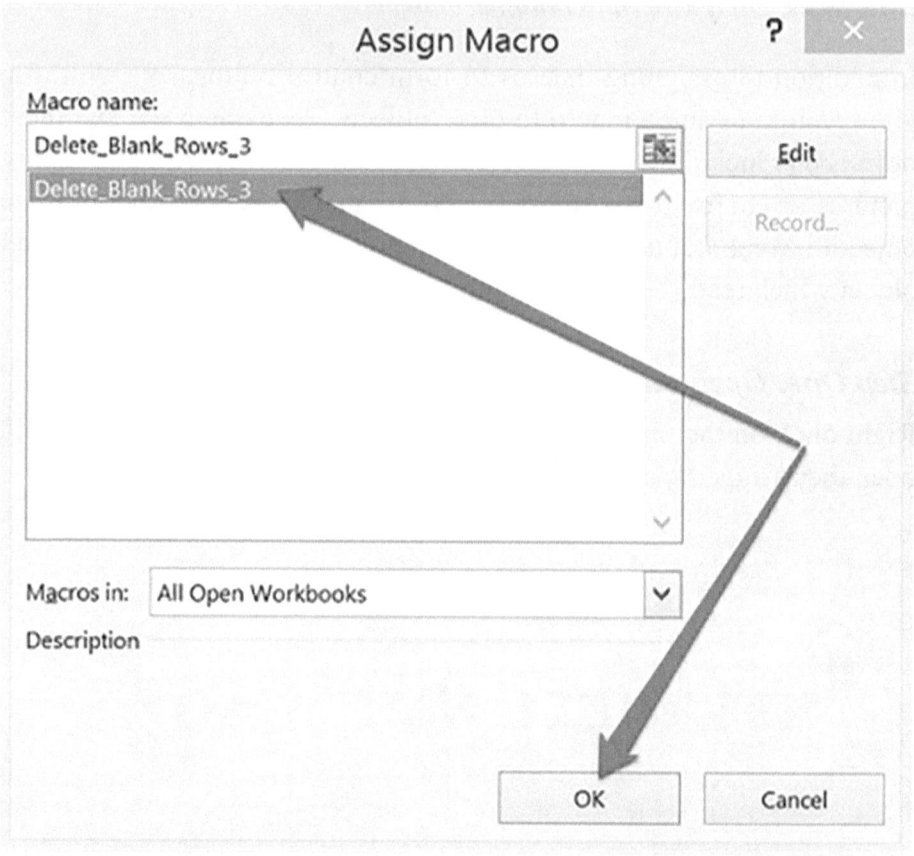

(https://powerspreadsheets.com/vba-sub-procedures/)

When you have finished the steps above, you can always execute the procedure by clicking on the relevant object.

Delete Blank Rows

(https://powerspreadsheets.com/vba-sub-procedures/)

Option Five: How to Execute A VBA Sub Procedure from another Procedure

Experts mention that most programmers use an existing procedure to execute a sub procedure. This process is called calling code since you are running a procedure to run an existing sub procedure point it is only when you call this procedure that the cold within the sub procedure is invoked. The calling code will always specify the correct irrelevant sub procedure and will transfer the control to that procedure. When the sub procedure has run the control will go back to the calling code or the main procedure.

Experts also say that there are many reasons why one should not call other procedures when running a sub procedure including the following:

This will help to reduce the size of the code and will also ensure that the code is crisp and clear for any other user to understand. It is also easier for you to debug, maintain or modify the code. Generally, it is a good idea to use this method to maintain several different procedures. You can use to create long procedures, but experts suggest that you avoid this. You should instead follow the suggestions of expert and create several small procedures, and write the main procedure to call all the small procedures. In the diagram below, you will see how it is easy to call upon several sub procedures using the main procedure. The main procedure is on the left side of the image while the sub procedures are on the right.

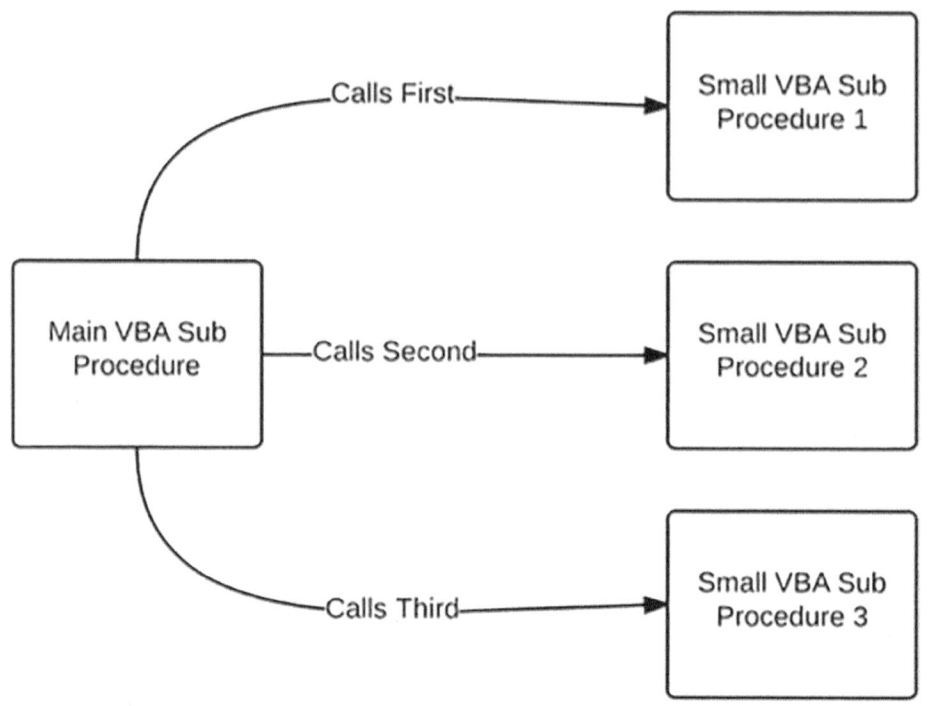

(https://powerspreadsheets.com/vba-sub-procedures/)

This will also help you avoid redundancies and repetition in the data. There are times when you will need to create a macro, which will carry out the same action in multiple places. In such cases, you can either create a sub procedure, which you will call in all those instances, or create a piece of code every time you need to call upon it. I am sure you know that it is easier and faster to use the same sub procedure across different applications of parts of the workbook.

If there are some procedures that you use often, you can store them in a module that you frequently used. When you do this you can import that sub procedure into every VBA project. When the module is imported you can call on the macros whenever required. The alternative to this is to copy and paste the code into a new VBA sub procedure point you will probably want to use the first option since it is easier and faster to implement in your work.

You can use any of the methods mentioned below to call A sub procedure from any other procedure or module letters look at these three methods in detail.

Method One: Use VBA Sub Procedure's Name

When you use this method, you will need to enter the following two things in the BBA cold where you are calling the sub procedure:

- The name of the procedure that you will be calling in the sub procedure.
- The argument that you will be using in the procedure will it be separated by commas.

In other words, the syntax that you will need to apply when I use this method is "Procedure_Name Arguments".

Latest assume that you will create a VBS the procedure, which will only call the Delete_Blank_Rows_3 macro.

The macro that we have written does not make sense because you can execute the Delete_Blank_Rows_3 macro directly. Since the structure is simple, we will use it as an example to see how the method works.

We have not developed a new sub procedure call calling Delete_Blank_Rows_3. This macro will only contain the following statements:

    Sub Calling_Delete_Blank_Rows()

    Delete_Blank_Rows_3

    End Sub

The image below will show you have the BBA code will appear in the visual basic editor environment.

```
Sub Calling_Delete_Blank_Rows()

    '
    ' Calling_Delete_Blank_Rows Macro
    ' Calls the Delete_Blank_Rows_3 macro.
    '
    ' Keyboard Shortcut: Ctrl+Shift+C
    '

    Delete_Blank_Rows_3

End Sub
```

(https://powerspreadsheets.com/vba-sub-procedures/)

You can always as a statement to the sub procedure to make it more useful and realistic.

Method Two: Use Call Statement

If you want to apply this method, you should proceed in the same fashion as method 1. In this case, you will also enter the name and the arguments of the procedure, which you will be calling within the VBA sub procedure.

There are two main differences between the methods 1 and 2:

1. In this method, you will need to use the call statement. This keyword will always be written ahead of the procedure you want to call.

2. In this method, arguments will always be enclosed in the parentheses.

In other words, if you use the second method you will need to apply the syntax "Call Procedure_Name (Arguments)".

Latest now locate how this will look in practice. We will create a simple VB A sub procedure and the sole purpose of this procedure is to call the Delete_Blank_Rows_3 macro. Latest call this new macro Delete_Blank_Rows_2. The syntax for this matter is given below:

>Sub Calling_Delete_Blank_Rows_2()

>Call Delete_Blank_Rows_3

>End Sub

The sub procedure will look as follows in the visual basic editor environment.

```
Sub Calling_Delete_Blank_Rows_2()

    '
    ' Calling_Delete_Blank_Rows_2 Macro
    ' Calls the Delete_Blank_Rows_3 macro.
    '
    ' Keyboard Shortcut: Ctrl+Shift+D
    '

    Call Delete_Blank_Rows_3

End Sub
```

>(https://powerspreadsheets.com/vba-sub-procedures/)

You may wonder why you would need to use a method where you should use the call keyword when you can use the previous method, which does not require the use of any keyword. One of the main reasons for using this method is that it provides clarity. Experts say that some programmers used the call keyword although it is optional to ensure that another procedure is being called whenever necessary.

Describe the above reasons expert suggest that you do not use the call keyword when running a sub procedure. According to the information found at the Microsoft development center, call statement is often used when a sub procedure does not begin with a specific identifier.

Method Three: Use The Application.Run Method

You should use the application.run method to execute the VBA sub procedure.

Experts suggest that you use this method if you want to call A sub procedure which has a name assigned to another variable. When you use the application.run method you can run the block of code in the sub procedure because you are passing the variable as an argument in the run method.

An example of this can be found in the book titled Excel 2013 power programming with VBA.

How to Call A VBA Sub Procedure from a Different Module

If you want to refer to A VBA sub procedure from other procedures, you will need to follow the process given below:

The search will first be carried out in the same module. If you do not find the VBA sub procedure in a module, you should look at the accessible procedures in different modules in the same workbook. If you want to call a procedure, which is private, both the procedures should be within the same module.

There will be cases where you have different procedures with the same name but in different modules. When you try to call one of the sub procedures by stating its name you will see that an error message is displayed.

This does not mean that you can always ask Excel to execute a procedure, which you want. To be more precise, you call a procedure, which is in a different module you have to clarify the following:

1. You should always state the name of the relevant module before you name the procedure.

2. You should always use a dot to separate the name of the sub procedure from the module.

You must use the following syntax in these cases: "Module_Name.Procedure_Name".

Now that you know how you should handle the cases where you have to call A sub procedure in a different module, you can choose to run the module in a different Excel workbook. Therefore we should now take a look at how to call a VBA sub procedure that is present in a different workbook.

How to Call A VBA Sub Procedure from a Different Excel Workbook

Experts say that there are two different ways in which excel will execute or run a sub procedure, which is stored in a different Excel workbook.

Build or establish a reference to different workbooks.

Specify the name of the workbook you explicitly want to refer to when you run the method.

Let us now look at how you can use either method for this purpose:

Method One: Establish A Reference To Another Excel Workbook.

You can create a reference to an Excel workbook using the following steps:

Step One: Open The References Dialog.

You should now go to the tools menu in the visual basic editor and select references.

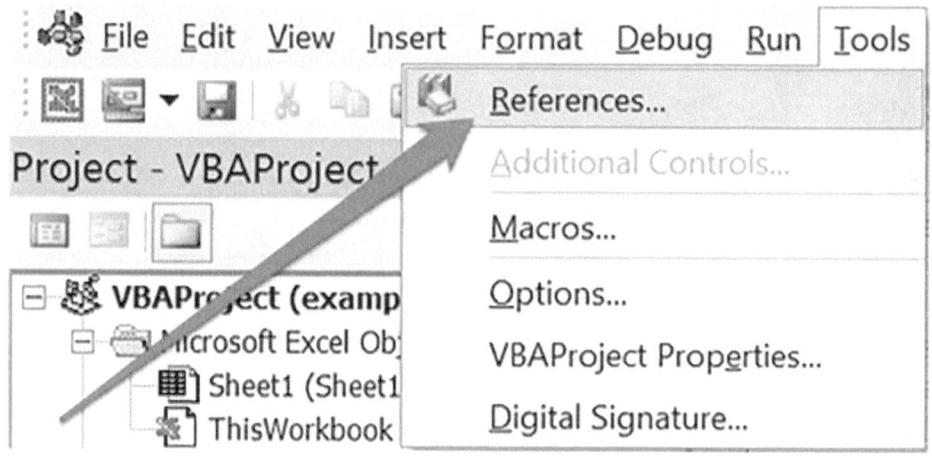

(htttps://powerspreadsheets.com/vba-sub-procedures/)

Step Two: Select The Excel Workbook To Add As Reference.

When you have completed the first step, Excel will display the reference dialog box.

This dialog box and provide all the references that you can use. The workbooks that are currently open are listed in that box. For example, look at the image below to see which Excel workbooks appear on the list.

In this case, every Excel workbook is not listed using its regular name. Instead, they will appear under the visual basic editor as their project names. Since every project name is VBAProject by default, the situation below is not very uncommon.

If you want to identify which VBA project you want to use as a reference, you can use the location data, which appears, at the bottom of the dialog box. Alternatively, you can always go back to the visual basic editor and change the name of the relevant project. If you want to add in Excel workbook, which is currently open, you should double click the name and select it. Then click on the ok button.

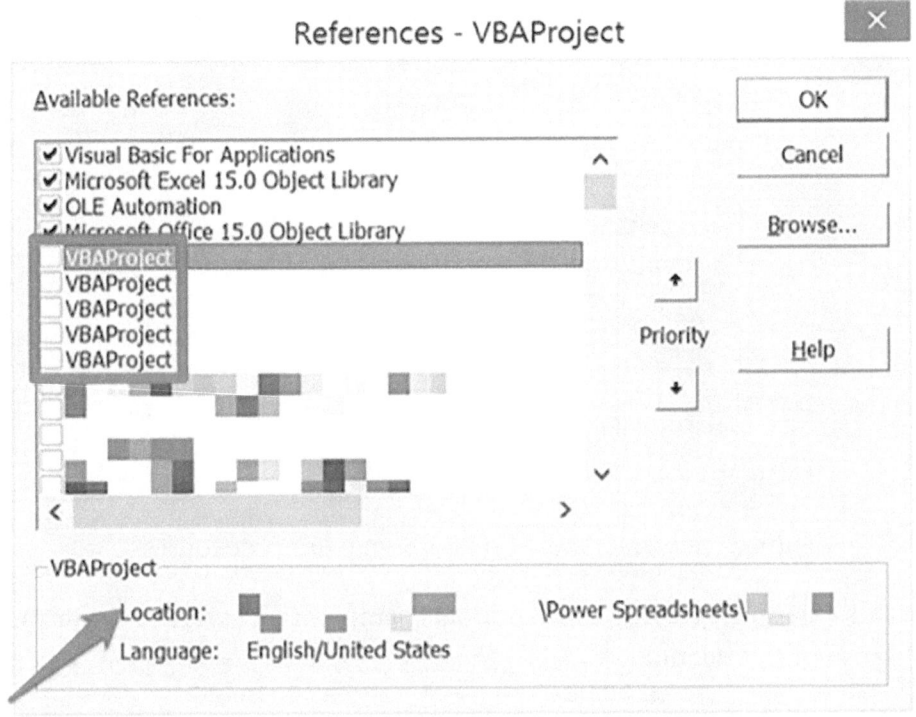

(https://powerspreadsheets.com/vba-sub-procedures/)

The references dialogue box only lists the Excel workbooks, which are open currently. You can also create a list of the references to workbooks, which are not currently open. To do this you will first need to click on the browse button on the right side in the references dialog box.

You see that the add reference dialog box is displayed. This box looks like every other dialogue box that you have used before. You should use the add reference dialog box to move to the folder where you have the relevant Excel workbook, selected workbook and then open it.

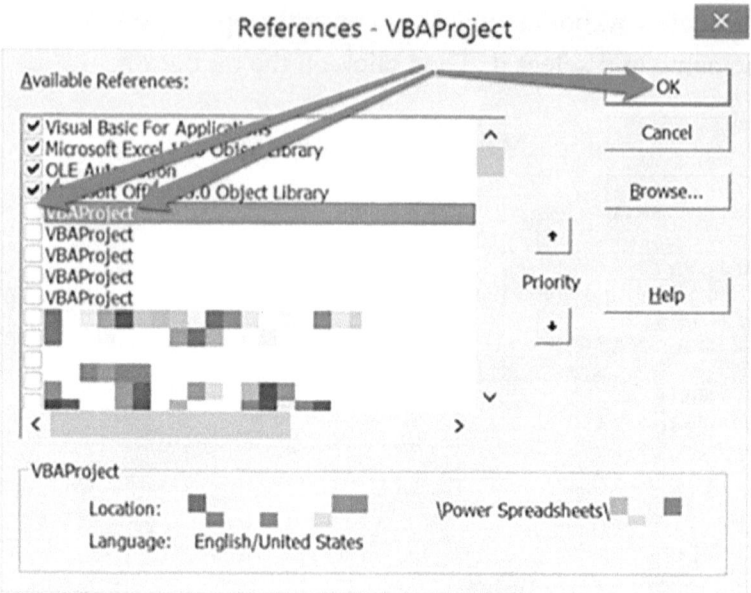

(https://powerspreadsheets.com/vba-sub-procedures/)

In this example below, we will add one sample Excel workbook for the purpose of this section.

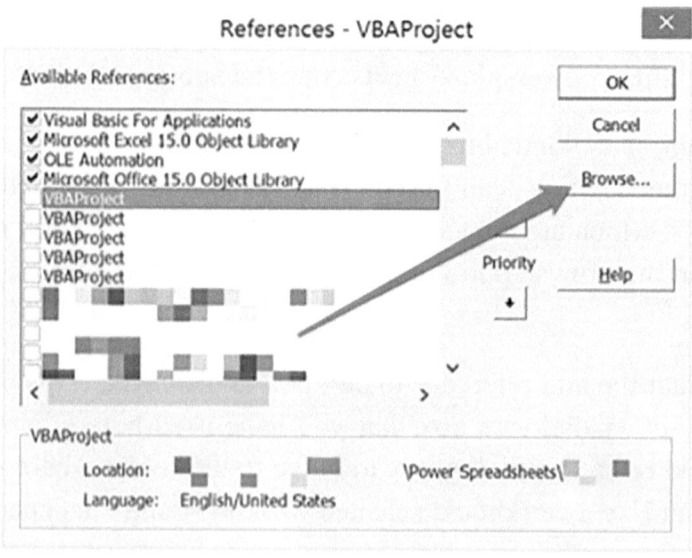

(https://powerspreadsheets.com/vba-sub-procedures/)

When you have completed the above step you will see that the relevant workbook is now I added to the bottom of the list of available references. You can then select the relevant reference and click ok. The references dialogue box will allow you to use this as the reference.

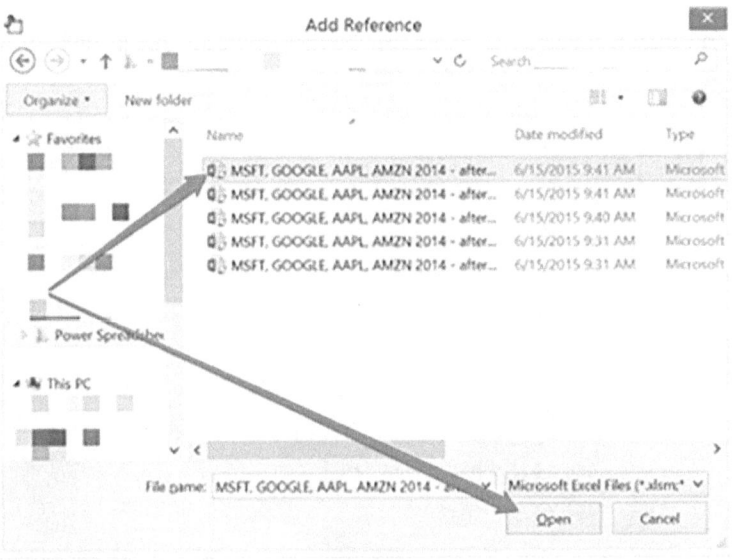

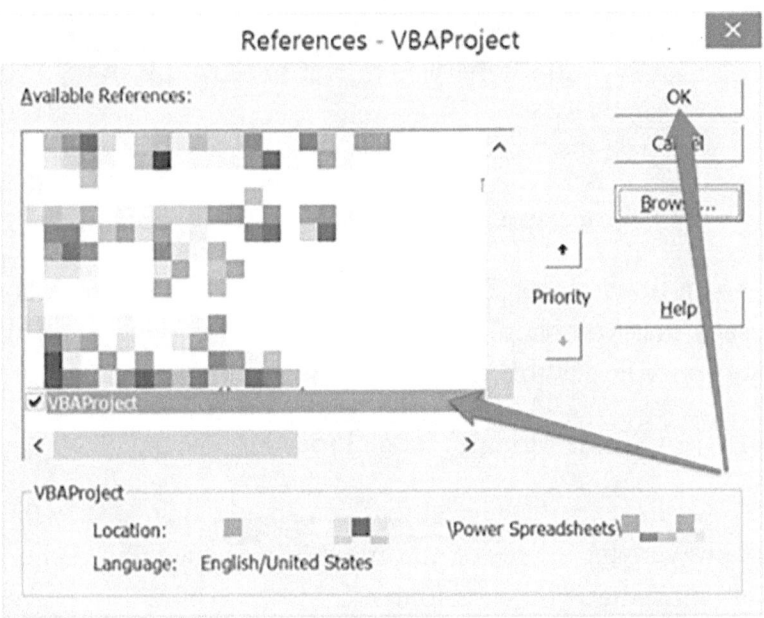

(https://powerspreadsheets.com/vba-sub-procedures/)

You are officially done. When you carry the steps mentioned above, the new reference that you have included will be listed in the project window in the visual basic editor. You can find this information in the references node. You can now prefer a call any procedures in a reference workbook as a divided the same workbook where you have written the sub procedure. This can be done by using a call keyword or the sub procedure's name.

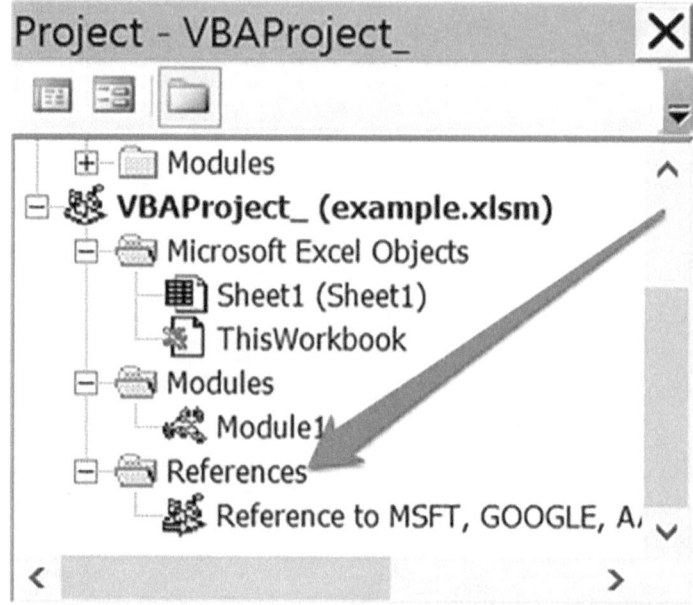

(https://powerspreadsheets.com/vba-sub-procedures/)

In the book titled Excel 2013 power programming with VB a, the author says that you should use the following syntax if you want to identify a procedure within another Excel workbook:

Project_Name.Module_Name.Procedure_Name

In simple words, experts suggest that you should first specify the name of your project, the name of the module and then the name of the actual sub procedure you want to use.

You will notice that when you open an Excel workbook, it will reference another workbook, which will be open automatically. Additional e you cannot close the referenced workbook without closing the originally opened workbook. If you try to do this excel will send you a warning message that this workbook is being referenced by another workbook and therefore cannot be closed.

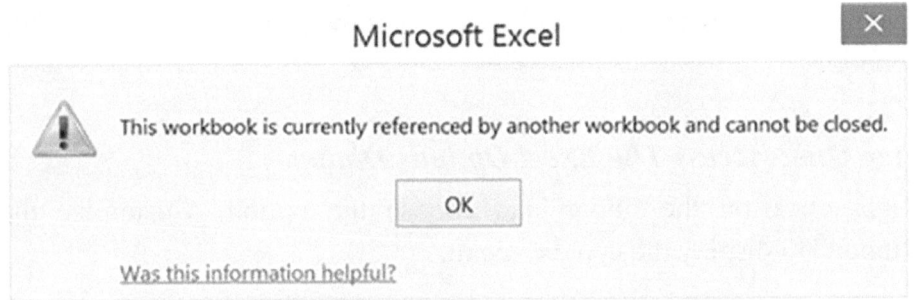

(https://powerspreadsheets.com/vba-sub-procedures/)

Method Two: Use The Application.Run Method.

You can use the application.run method to execute any VBA sub procedure. If you want to use this method, you do not have to create a reference as explained in the previous section. You must, however, have the Excel workbook, which contains a sub procedure open. To see an example of how you can use this method, please refer to the book titled 'Excel 2013 Power Programming with VBA'.

Option Six: How to Execute A VBA Sub Procedure Using the Ribbon

If you want to include a button to the ribbon which points to a relevant sub procedure, you should follow the steps below. You can execute the macro by clicking on the button in the Ribbon.

In this section, we will look at how you can add a button to the ribbon, and what you should do to run the macro or the block of code within that sub procedure. We will continue to use the Delete_Blank_Rows_3 macro for our example. This is the most appropriate method that one can use for a macro that is present in the personal workbook.

The personal workbook is where you will store the relevant macros that you can use in an Excel workbook. In simple words, the macros that are stored in the personal workbook can be called upon or used regardless of which excel workbook you are working on. Let us look at five simple steps that you will need to follow to add the button to the Ribbon.

Step One: Access The Excel Options Dialog.

Right click on the ribbon and choose the option "Customize the Ribbon" to display the context menu.

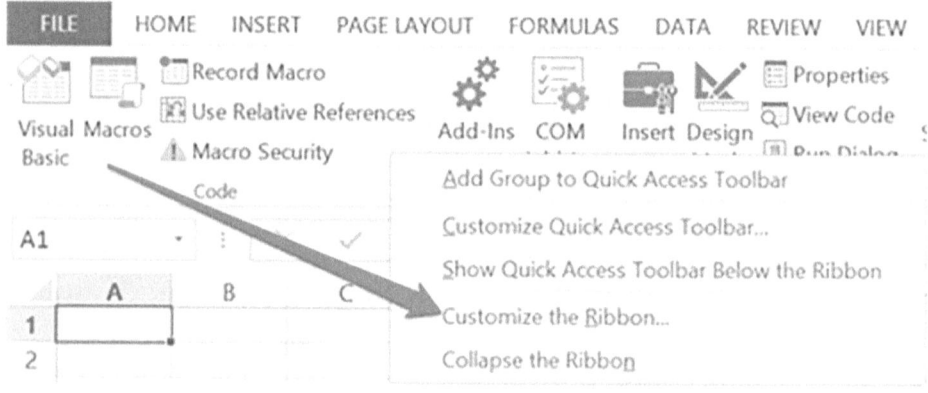

(https://powerspreadsheets.com/vba-sub-procedures/)

Step Two: Choose To Work With Macros.

In the Excel Options dialog box, you can choose the commands you want to include to the ribbon from the drop-down menu in the customize ribbon tab.

(https://powerspreadsheets.com/vba-sub-procedures/)

You can browse through different commands before you add them to the Ribbon. All you need to do is click the command, and then select "Macros."

(https://powerspreadsheets.com/vba-sub-procedures/)

When you have done this, you will see a list of all the macros that you can include in the Ribbon. This list will be found in the Choose commands list, and will appear below the choose commands drop down menu. Please see the image below for a better understanding.

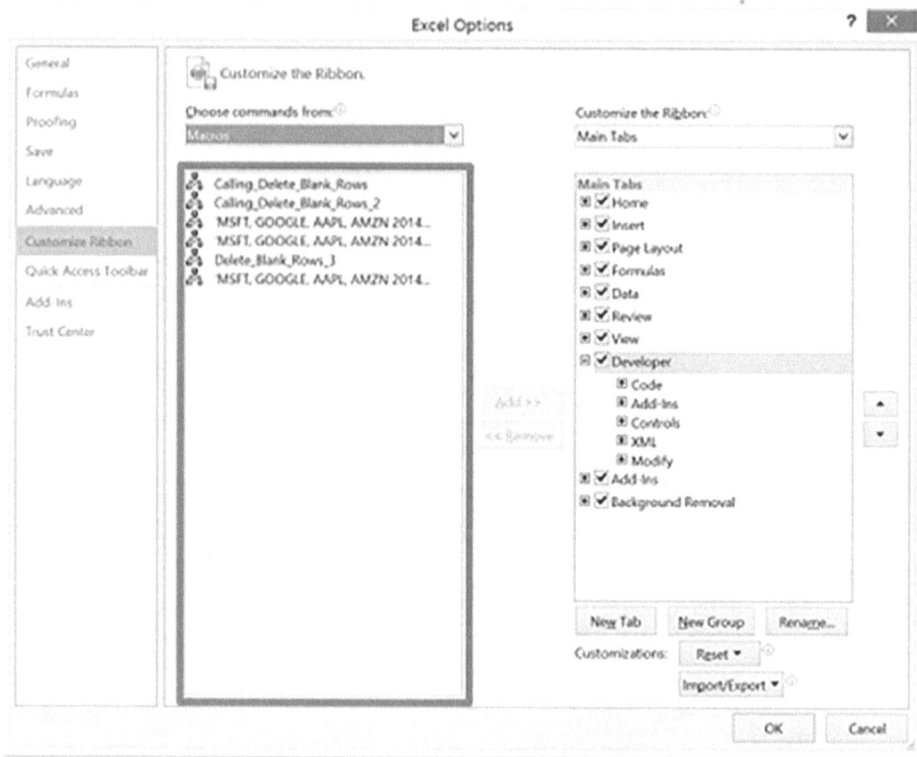

(https://powerspreadsheets.com/vba-sub-procedures/)

Step Three: Select The Tab And Group Of Commands To Which You Want To Add The Macro.

You can find the Customize the Ribbon list on the right side in the Excel Options dialog box. This is where you will find the list of all the commands that can be found in the Ribbon. You will notice that these commands are organized by groups of commands and tabs.

The image below will show you how there are five groups of commands, namely Add-Ins, Code, XML, Modify and Controls in the

Developer Tab. You can choose where to add the macro button to the ribbon in the "Customize the Ribbon" List. You can also expand or contract a tab in Excel or any group of commands using the plus and minus signs that appear in the list on the left side. You can now include new command groups or tabs to the Excel workbook using the buttons in the Customize Ribbon list dialog box.

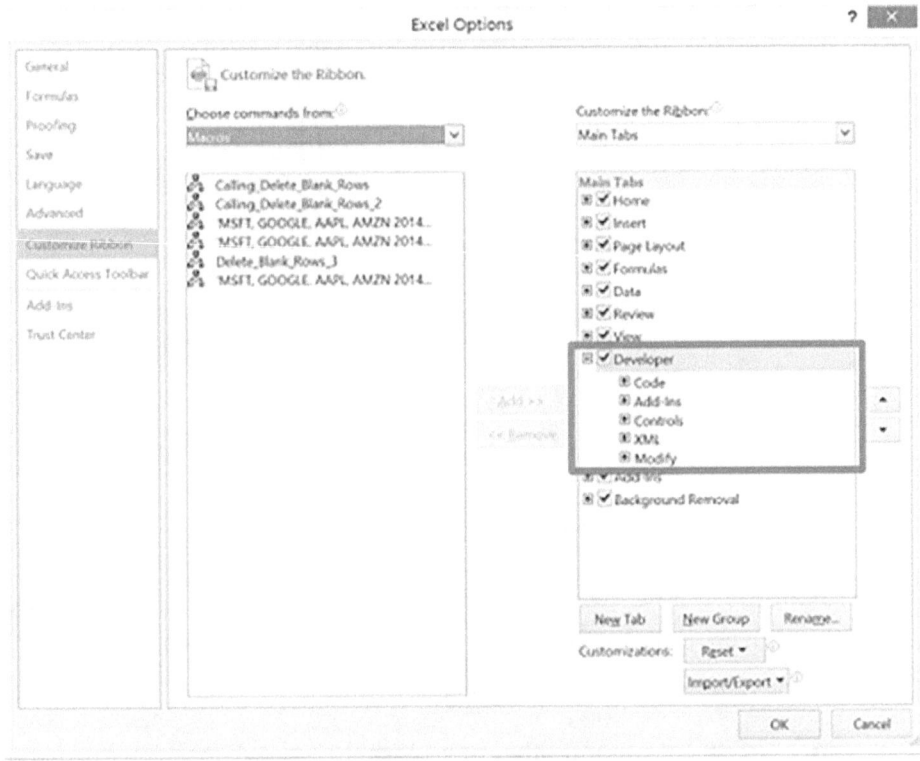

(https://powerspreadsheets.com/vba-sub-procedures/)

You can now choose to create a new command group or choose an existing command group when you want to add a macro to the Ribbon. In the section below, we will talk about how you can add a new group of commands and tab to the ribbon.

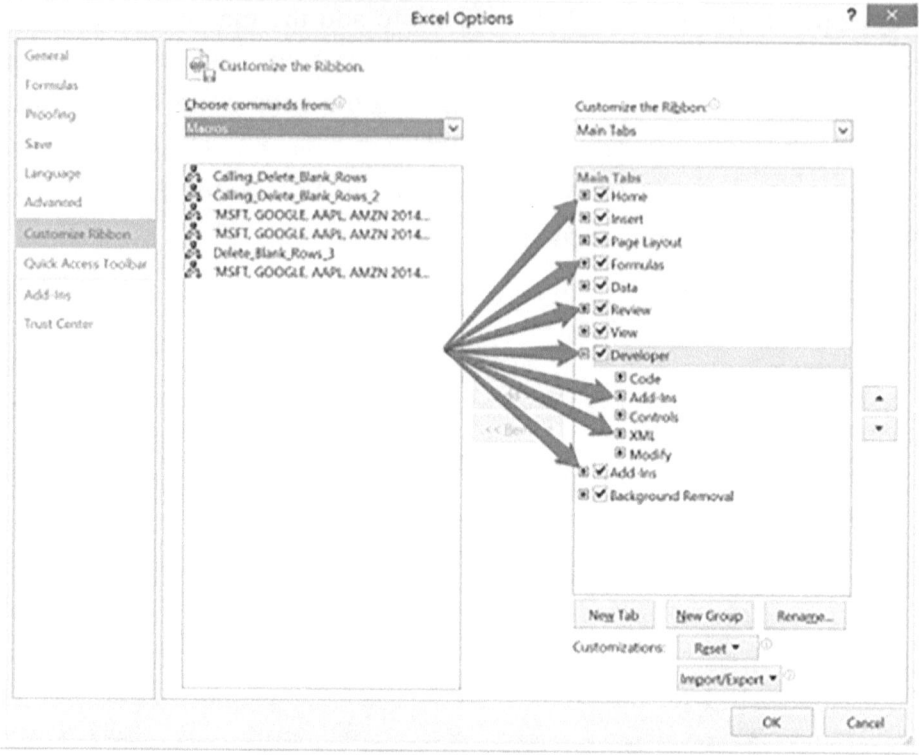

(https://powerspreadsheets.com/vba-sub-procedures/)

In the example below, we will add a new tab immediately after the Developer tab in Excel. To do this, you should go to the "Developer" Tab and click the "New Tab" button.

You can choose to rename the newly included tab by clicking the Rename button. Excel will now display the Rename dialog box. You should enter the name of the collection and click OK. You must repeat this process for the command group. You should first select the "New Group (Custom)" option and then rename the button.

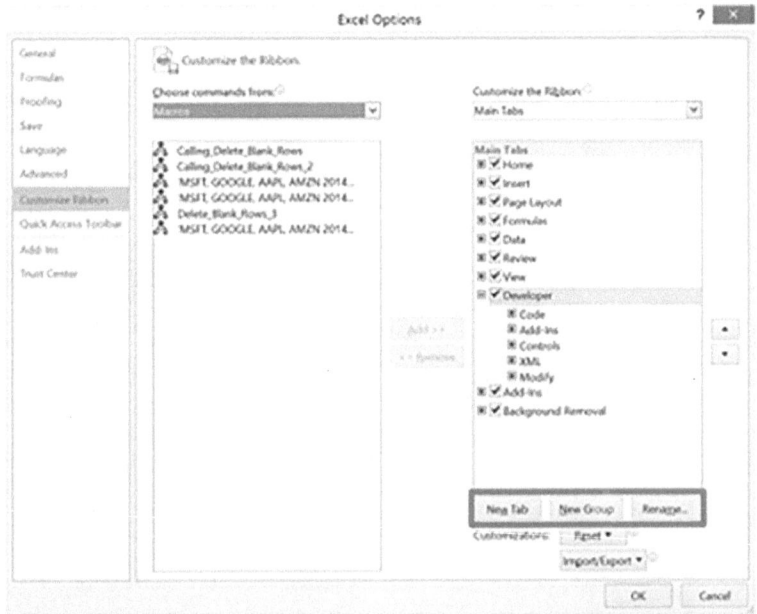

(https://powerspreadsheets.com/vba-sub-procedures/)

(https://powerspreadsheets.com/vba-sub-procedures/)

(https://powerspreadsheets.com/vba-sub-procedures/)

Excel will display a different rename box, which will allow you to choose the name or a symbol that will represent the group of command.

(https://powerspreadsheets.com/vba-sub-procedures/)

You can choose an icon if you want. In this example, we will choose an icon and then enter the name for the command group. Click OK once you are sure of the changes.

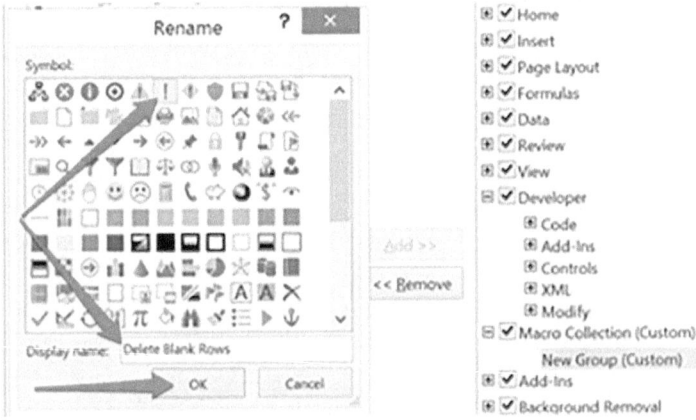

(https://powerspreadsheets.com/vba-sub-procedures/)

When all the steps are in order, you should choose the group of commands that you wish to include in the macro. In the example below, the Delete Blank Rows group is the command group that has just been created.

(https://powerspreadsheets.com/vba-sub-procedures/)

Step Four: Add VBA Sub Procedure To The Ribbon.

When you want to add a macro button to the ribbon, you should select the relevant macro from choose commands list and hit the Add button, which is present in the center of the dialog box. The image below will show you how you can add the Delete_Blank_Rows_3 macro to the ribbon.

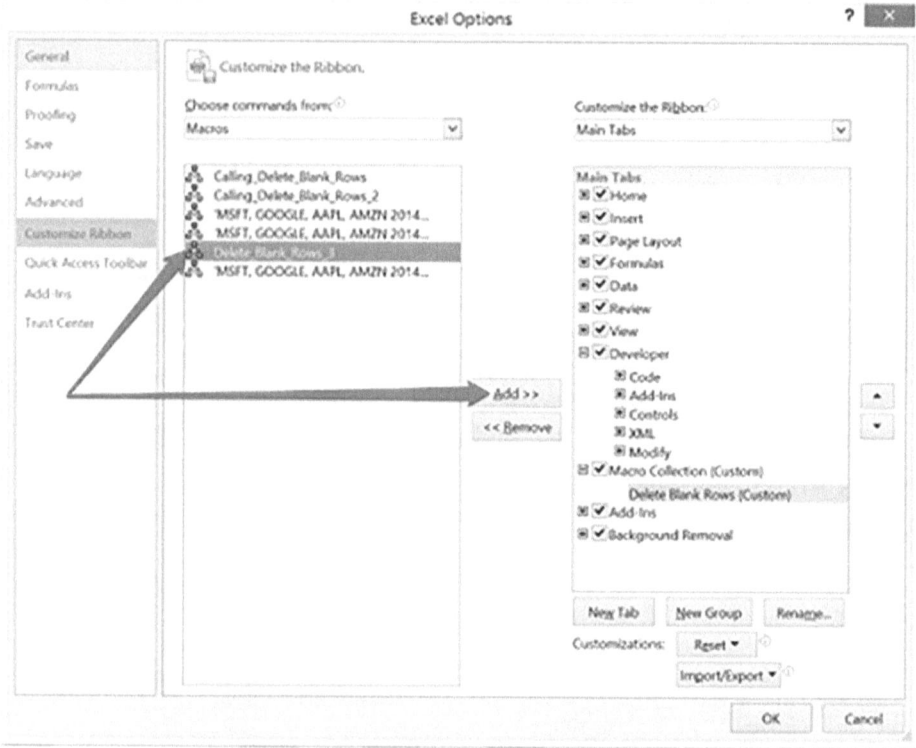

(https://powerspreadsheets.com/vba-sub-procedures/)

Step Five: Finish The Process.

To complete the process, you should click OK which is found at the bottom right corner of the dialog box.

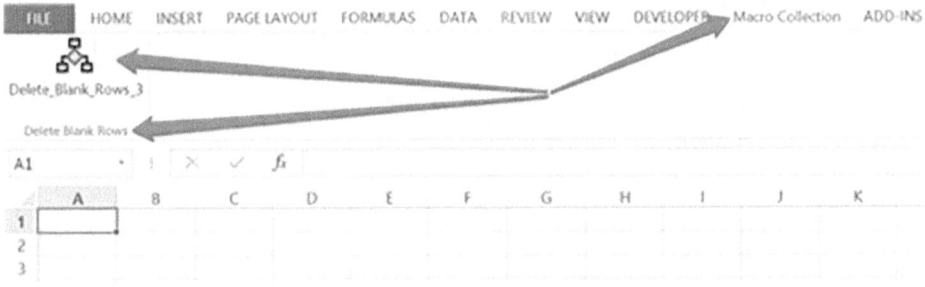

(https://powerspreadsheets.com/vba-sub-procedures/)

Excel will now close the Excel Options dialog box and make the necessary changes. You will notice that in the case of this example, there is already a new tab, called Macro Collections that has been included. You will also see that a group of commands and a button have been included to the ribbon.

(https://powerspreadsheets.com/vba-sub-procedures/)

83

When you complete this process, you can execute the macro or the sub procedure by simply clicking on the correct button in the Ribbon. Excel will enable this icon even if the workbook that has the macro in it is closed. If the relevant workbook is closed, Excel will open that workbook with the macro in it, before it executes the code.

Option Seven: How to Execute A VBA Sub Procedure Using the Quick Access Toolbar

You can find the Quick Access Toolbar on the upper left corner in your Excel workbook.

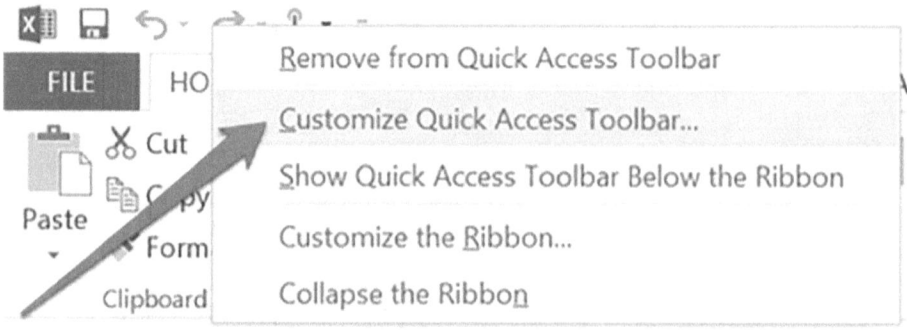

(https://powerspreadsheets.com/vba-sub-procedures/)

Just like we did with Ribbon, you can make some changes to the Quick Access Toolbar to include a button that is assigned to the sub procedure. This means that you can execute the code in the procedure by simply clicking that button.

You should use this method only when the macro you are including to the quick access toolbar is found in your personal workbook. It is the same as the method of using the ribbon to execute the sub procedure. You should also remember that if you include the macro to the Quick Access toolbar, you can also ensure that this button only appears in the Excel workbook that has the macro written in it.

We will look at how you can use the quick access toolbar and how you can customize it for this purpose. Let us first look at how you can add a macro button to the toolbar in five simple steps.

Step One: Access the Excel Options Dialog

In the previous sections, you have learned how you can access the Options dialog box, and this section provides some additional information that you can use. For this specific example, it is always a good idea to access the Quick Access Toolbar tab using the Excel Options dialog box. All you need to do is right-click on the Quick Access toolbar and select the option to "Customize Quick Access Toolbar." When you complete this step, you will see the Options Dialog box open in front of you.

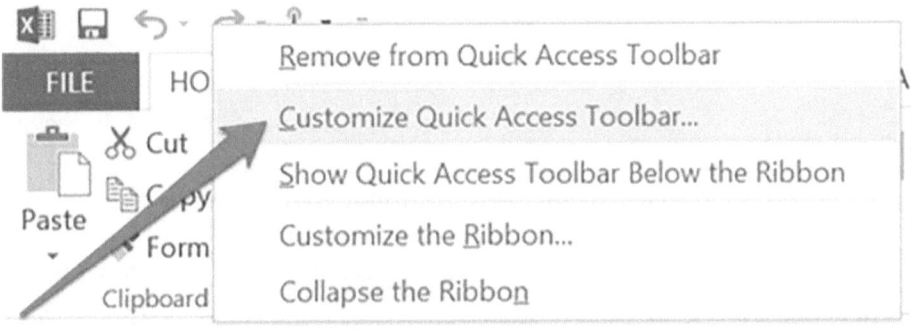

(https://powerspreadsheets.com/vba-sub-procedures/)

Step Two: Choose For Which Excel Workbooks The Customized Quick Access Toolbar Applies.

You will see a drop-down menu in the top right corner of the excel options dialog box. This drop-down menu is for the Quick Access toolbar. You should navigate to the section where you can make some changes to which workbooks should reflect the change you make. Choose your preferred option from the drop-down menu in the Customize Quick Access dialog box.

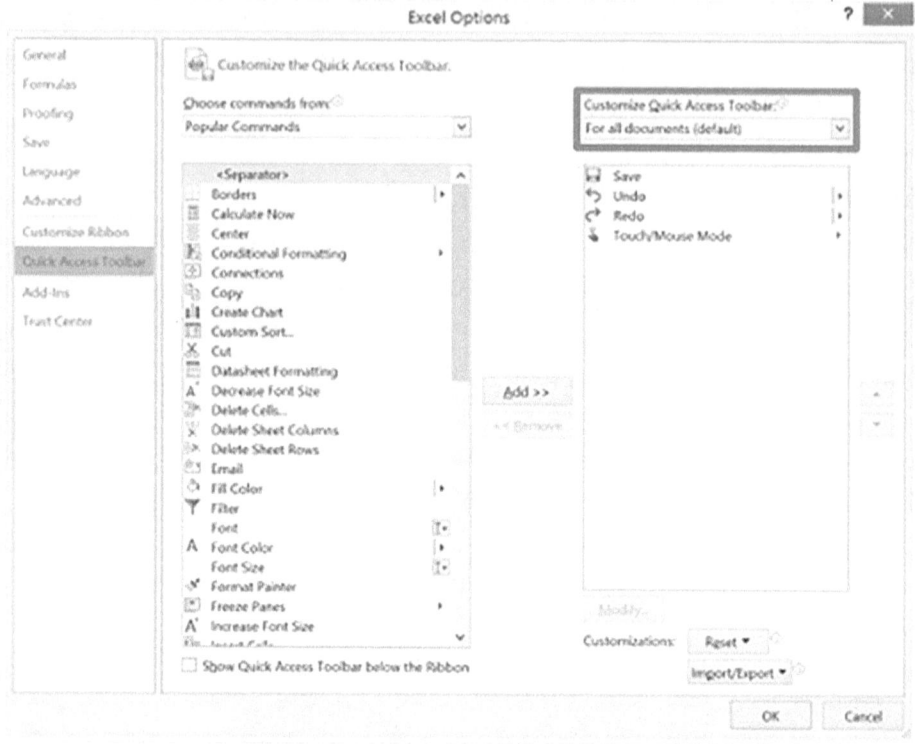

(https://powerspreadsheets.com/vba-sub-procedures/)

If you want this button to appear in every Excel workbook, you should choose the option "For all documents (default). This is the default setting that will be applied to every workbook.

If you want the button to appear only in one workbook, you should choose the name of the workbook. The image below shows a section of the options that you can find in the drop-down menu in the Customize Quick Access Toolbar section.

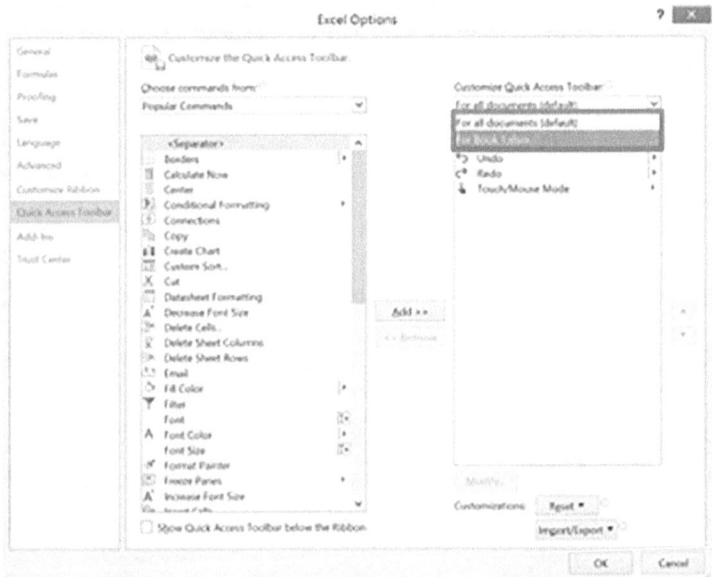

(https://powerspreadsheets.com/vba-sub-procedures/)

In this example, we only have the workbook named "Book 1" open on the system. In this example, we will use the default option. This customization will apply to ever workbook that you open.

(https://powerspreadsheets.com/vba-sub-procedures/)

Step Three: Choose To Work With Macros.

In the Excel Options dialog box, you should navigate to the top left corner in the Quick Access toolbar. Here, you will find the choose commands option in the drop-down menu. Select "Macros" from the drop-down list.

Step Four: Add Macro To Quick Access Toolbar.

Once you complete the step above, you will see a list of all the macros in your Excel workbook in the options dialog box. These are the macros that you can include to the Quick Access Toolbar. These macros will be in the choose Commands list on the left side of the Quick Acess toolbar tab in the dialog box.

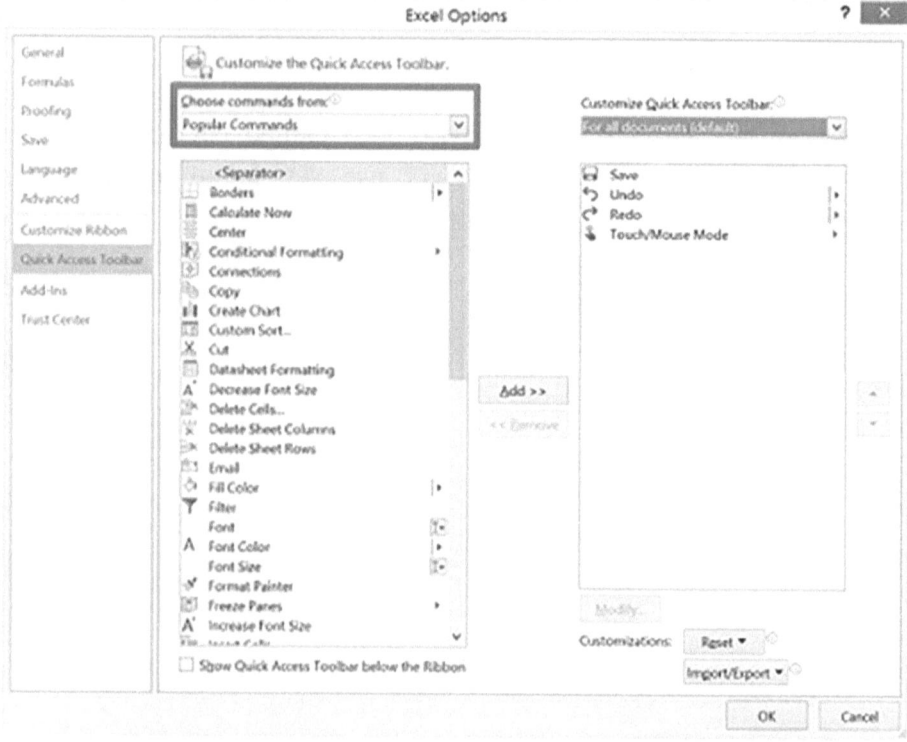

(https://powerspreadsheets.com/vba-sub-procedures/)

You should now choose the macro that you want to include from the Choose Commands option in the list box. Click on Add button, which will appear in the center of the Options dialog box. The image below will show you how you should include the Delete_Blank_Rows_3 macro.

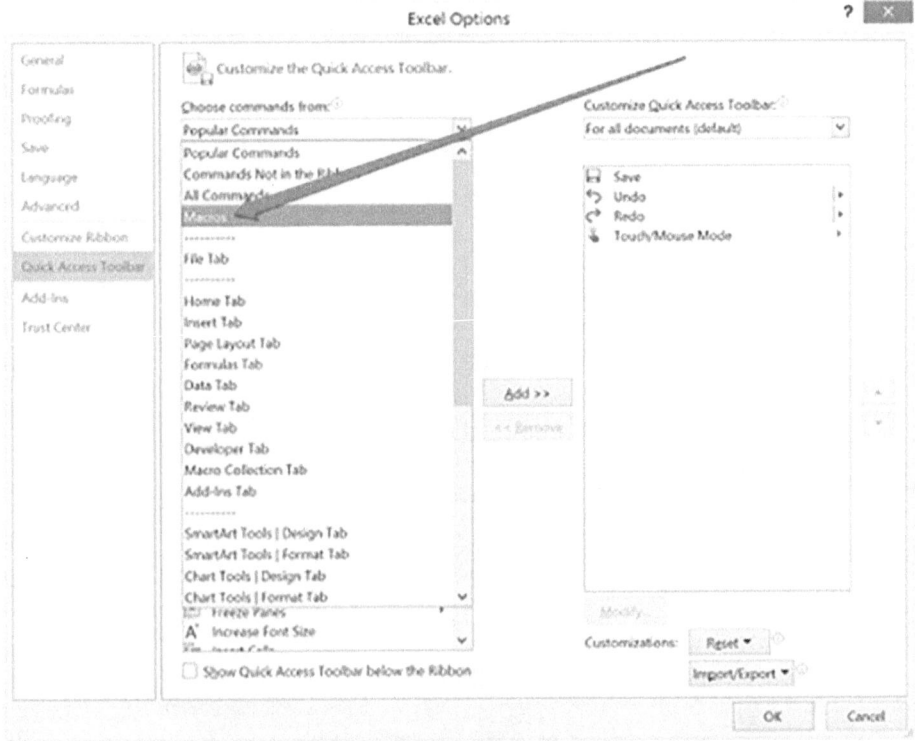

(https://powerspreadsheets.com/vba-sub-procedures/)

Step Five: Click The OK Button.

Once you run the first four steps, you will see the macro button in the Quick Access Toolbar. You will see that this button is found in the Customize Quick Access Toolbar list. This list is found on the right side of the options dialog box. You should now press the OK button at the bottom right corner of the options dialog box to complete the process. This will implement the necessary changes.

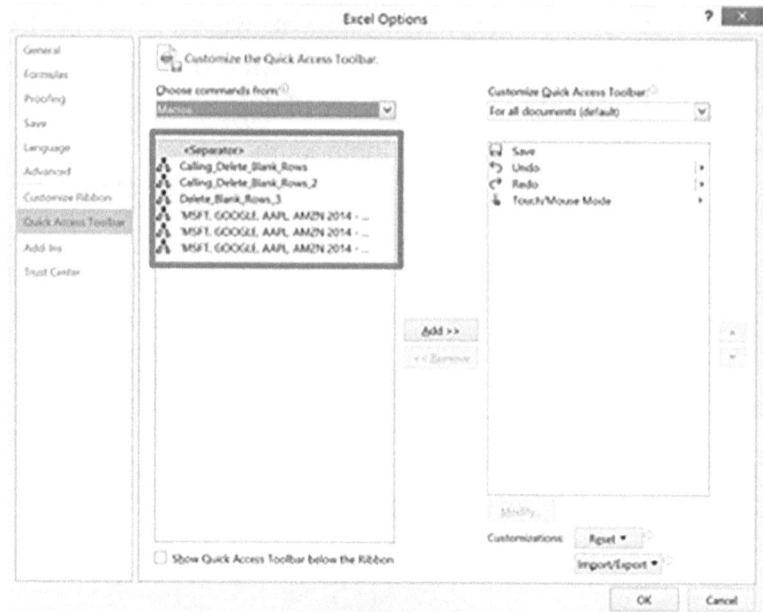

(https://powerspreadsheets.com/vba-sub-procedures/)

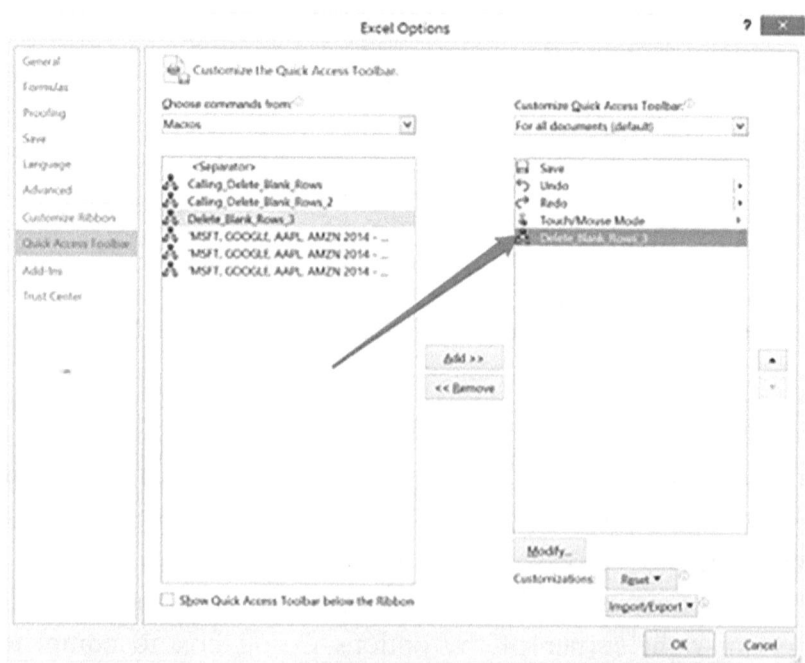

(https://powerspreadsheets.com/vba-sub-procedures/)

When you move back to Excel, you will see that the necessary macro button has been included in the Quick Access Toolbar. To run or execute the sub procedure, you can click on the button that you added to the Quick Access toolbar.

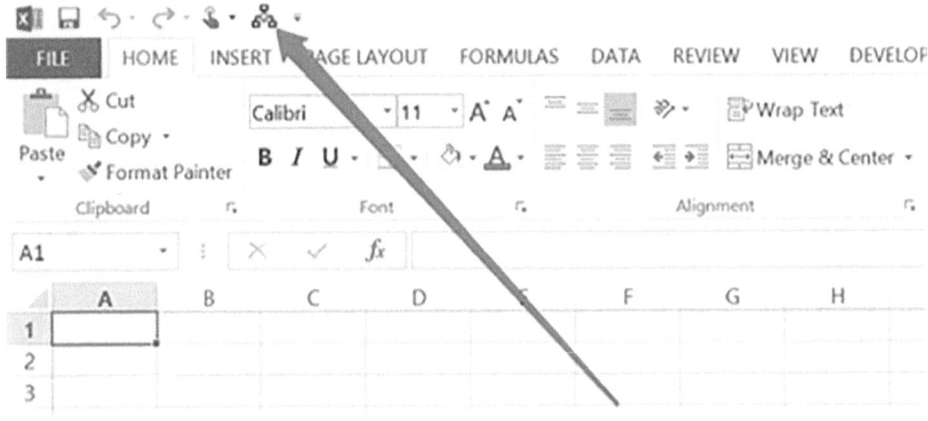

(https://powerspreadsheets.com/vba-sub-procedures/)

Option Eight: How to Execute A VBA Sub Procedure When a Particular Event Occurs

You can run a specific VBA Sub procedure in Excel even when an event occurs. Excel will check with you if the sub procedure should run, and you can either choose to ignore the procedure or ignore the event. In the book titled, 'Excel 2013 Power Programming With VBA,' the author talks about several events where you may come across this issue:

1. Entering information in a worksheet
2. Opening a workbook
3. Clicking a command button
4. Saving a file

A VBA Sub procedure that is executed even when an event occurs is called an event handler procedure. This type of procedure has two characteristics that separate it from the other Sub procedures in VBA.

The name of this sub procedure will always have a different structure. Their name will need to stick to the following syntax – "object_EventName." The names of such procedures will have three elements:

1. Objects
2. Underscore
3. Name of the event

The module for the object in the name is the VBA module in which this sub procedure is written or stored. It is important to learn more about event handler procedures, and this is an extensive topic to cover. To learn more about this topic, you should refer to chapter seventeen in the book titled 'Excel 2013 Power Programming With VBA.'

Option Nine: Executing the VBA Sub Procedure Using the Immediate Window

It is a good idea to execute a sub procedure in VBA using the immediate window in the environment. It is always a good idea to do this if you are building an application in the visual basic environment. The Immediate Window can be found at the bottom section of the Visual Basic Editor.

If you're finding the information valuable so far, please be sure to leave 5-star feedback on Amazon

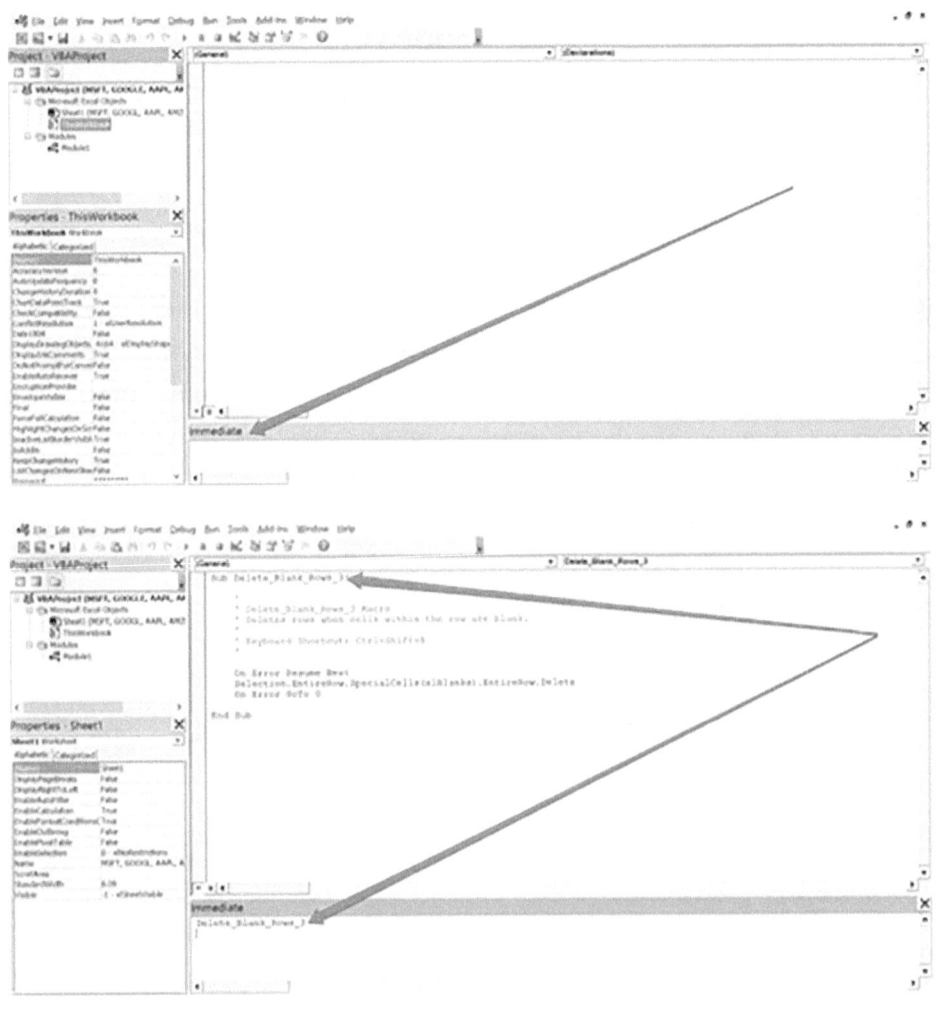

(https://powerspreadsheets.com/vba-sub-procedures/)

To learn more about the Immediate Window, please read the first few books of the series. You can also learn more about the IDE in VBA in those books. If you want to run a sub procedure in VBA in the Immediate Window, you should type the name of that procedure in the window and click Enter. To conclude, the concept of procedures and sub procedures is used frequently in most blogs and books that cover VBA and macros. It is important for you to understand what these terms mean if you want to become an expert in VBA.

Conclusion

Thank you for purchasing the book. If you want to master VBA, there are some concepts that you should know well. You should also have some tricks and tips up your sleeve to help you overcome any problems you may have with VBA. This book will help you master some of the concepts, and also leave you with some tips that you can use to troubleshoot and handle any errors and exceptions.

I hope the information in the book will help you improve your VBA programming skills.

P.S. If you don't mind, please drop a short review of my title on Amazon and feel free to tell me what you think! Thanks a lot!

Will You Help Me?

Hi there, avid reader! If you have extra time on your hands, I would really, really appreciate it if you could take a moment to click my author profile in Amazon. In there, you will find all the titles I authored and who knows, you might find more interesting topics to read and learn!

If it's not too much to ask, you can also leave and write a review for all the titles that you have read – whether it's a positive or negative review. An honest and constructive review of my titles is always welcome and appreciated since it will only help me moving forward in creating these books. There will always be room to add or improve, or sometimes even subtract certain topics, that is why these reviews are always important for us. They will also assist other avid readers, professionals who are looking to sharpen their knowledge, or even newbies to any topic, in their search for the book that caters to their needs the most.

If you don't want to leave a review yourself, you can also vote on the existing reviews by voting Helpful (Thumbs Up) or Unhelpful (Thumbs Down), especially on the top 10 or so reviews.

If you want to go directly to the vote or review process, please visit my author file page in Amazon for my below titles:

> Machine Learning For Beginners : A Comprehensive, Step-by-Step Guide to Learning and Understanding Machine Learning Concepts, Technology and Principles for Beginners . Audiobook format is also available at www.audible.com

> Machine Learning : A Comprehensive, Step-by-Step Guide to Intermediate Concepts and Techniques in Machine Learning

Machine Learning : A Comprehensive, Step-by-Step Guide to Learning and Applying Advanced Concepts and Techniques in Machine Learning

Excel VBA : A Step-By-Step Tutorial For Beginners To Learn Excel VBA Programming From Scratch . Audiobook format is also available at www.audible.com

Excel VBA : Intermediate Lessons in Excel VBA Programming for Professional Advancement . Audiobook format is also available at www.audible.com

Excel VBA: A Step-By-Step Comprehensive Guide on Advanced Excel VBA Programming Techniques and Strategies

Again, I truly appreciate the time and effort that you will be putting in leaving a review for my titles or even just for voting. This will only inspire me to create more quality content and titles in the future.

Thank you and have a great day!

Peter Bradley

Sources

https://www.dummies.com/software/microsoft-office/excel/10-resources-for-excel-vba-help/

https://techcommunity.microsoft.com/t5/Excel/9-quick-tips-to-improve-your-VBA-macro-performance/td-p/173687

http://what-when-how.com/excel-vba/ten-vba-tips-and-tricks/

https://www.tutorialspoint.com/vba/vba_sub_procedure.htm

https://powerspreadsheets.com/vba-sub-procedures/

https://docs.microsoft.com/en-us/office/vba/language/concepts/getting-started/calling-sub-and-function-procedures

https://www.excelfunctions.net/vba-functions-and-subroutines.html

https://powerspreadsheets.com/vba-sub-procedures/

www.ingramcontent.com/pod-product-compliance
Lightning Source LLC
Chambersburg PA
CBHW021450210526
45463CB00002B/714